50 animal mandalas coloring book for adults

stress- relief

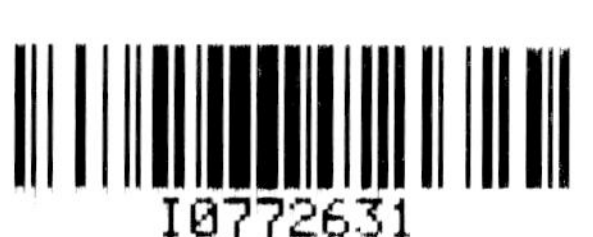

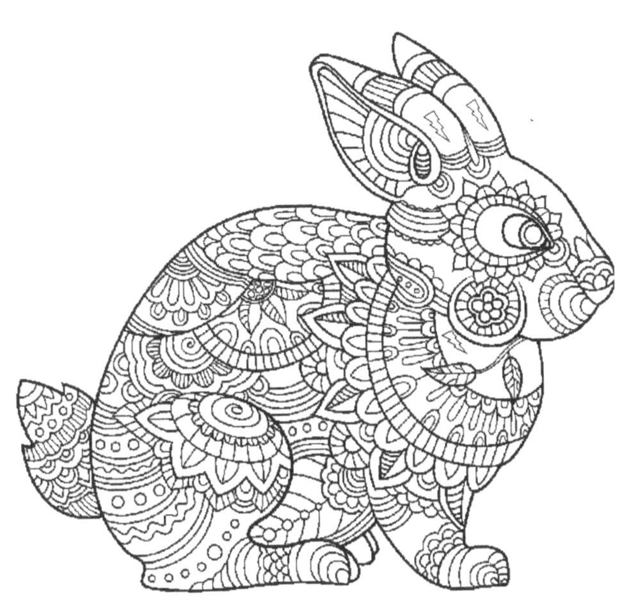

this book
belongs to

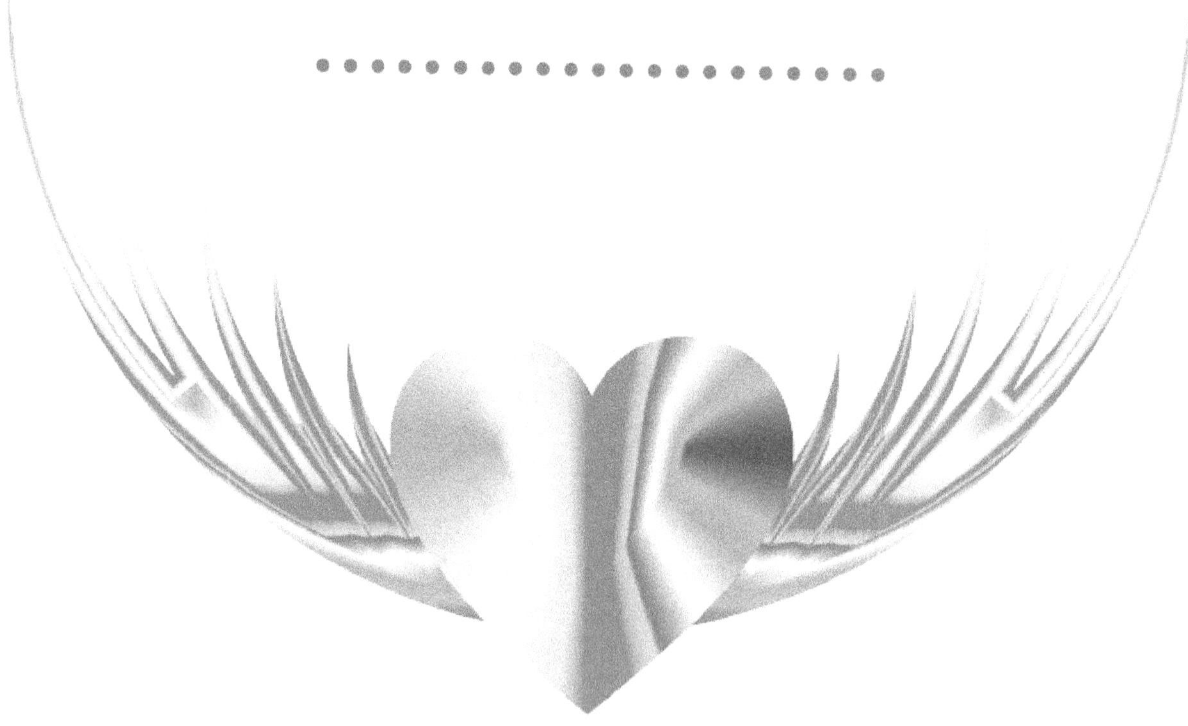

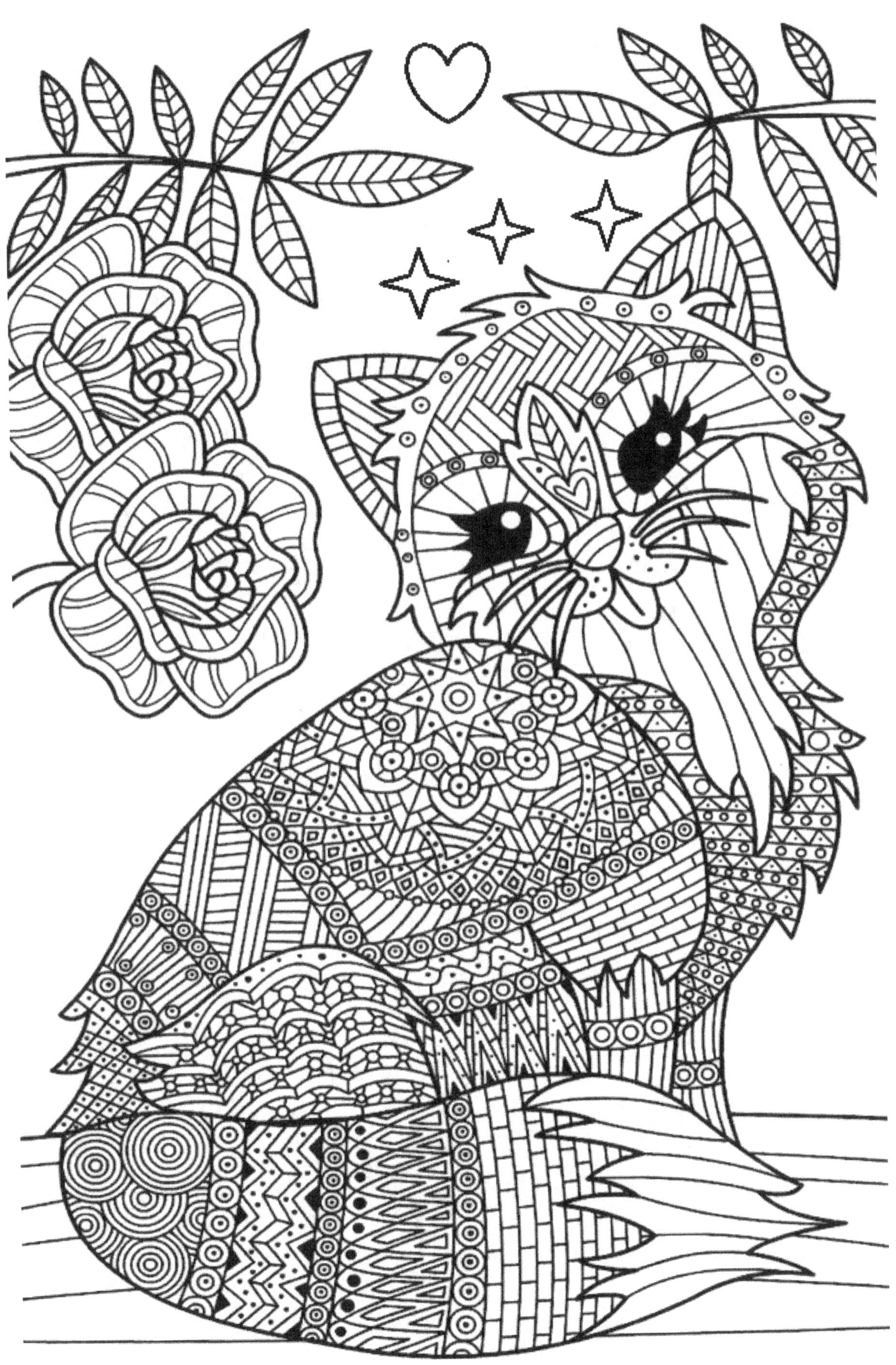

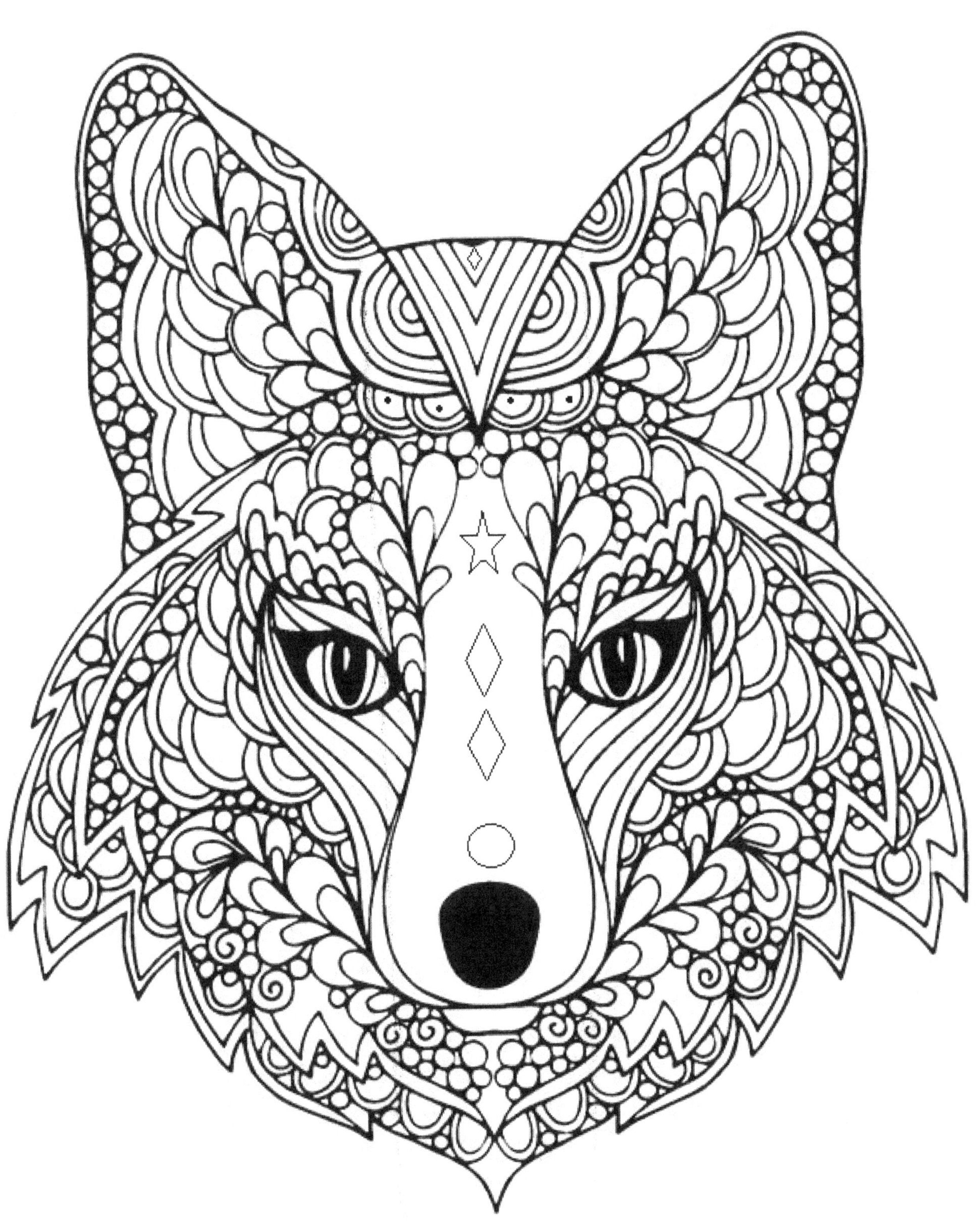

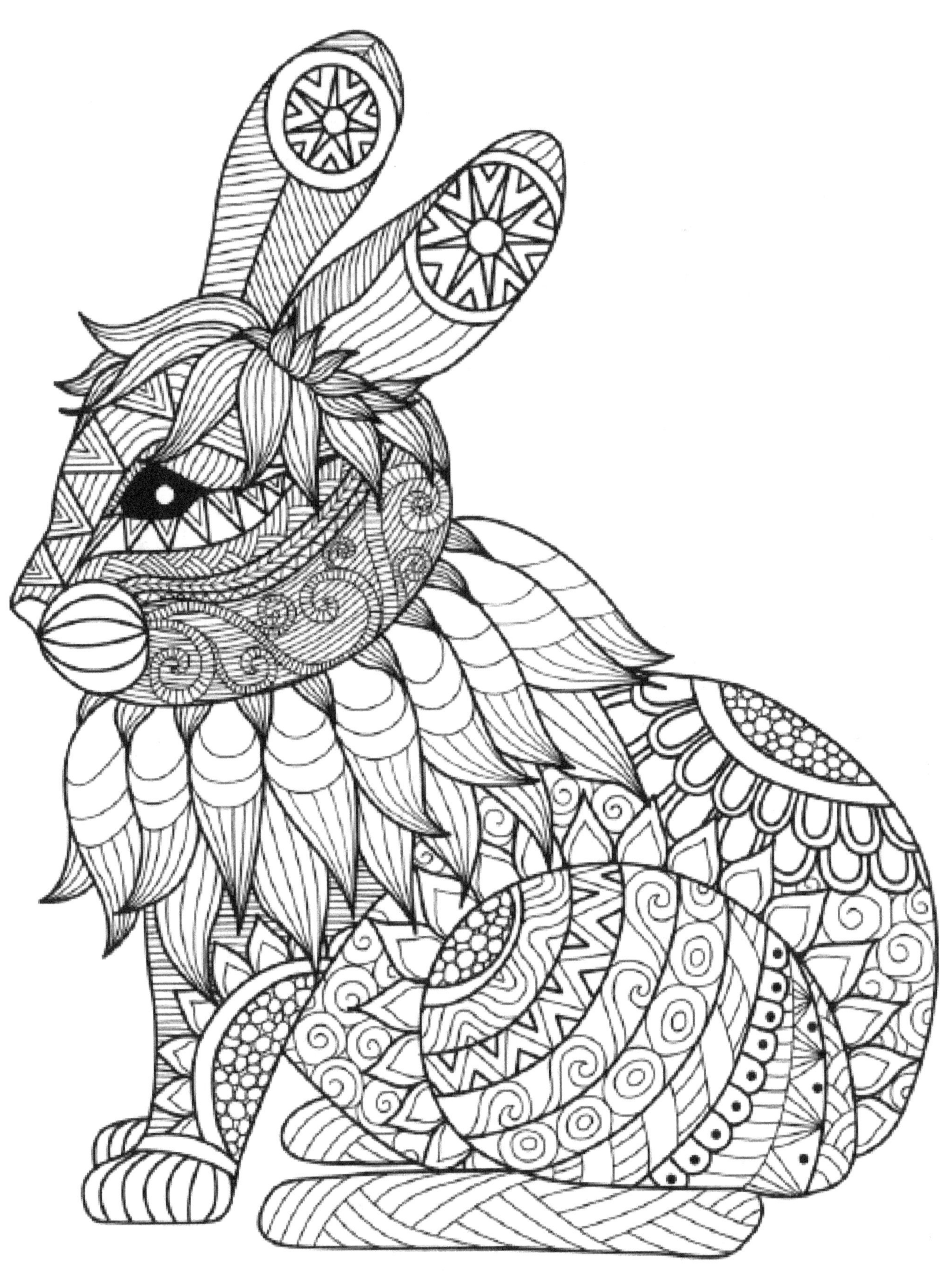

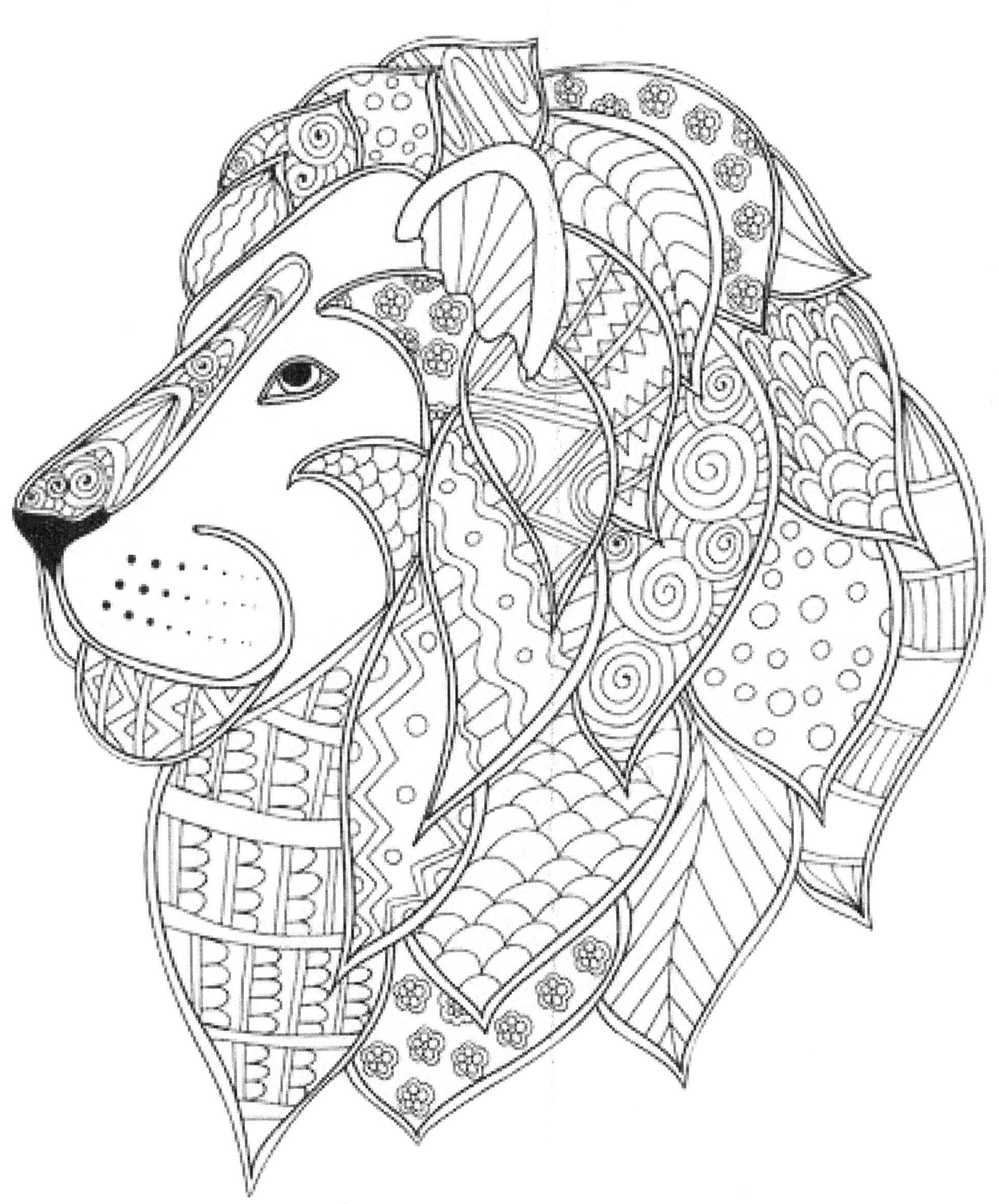

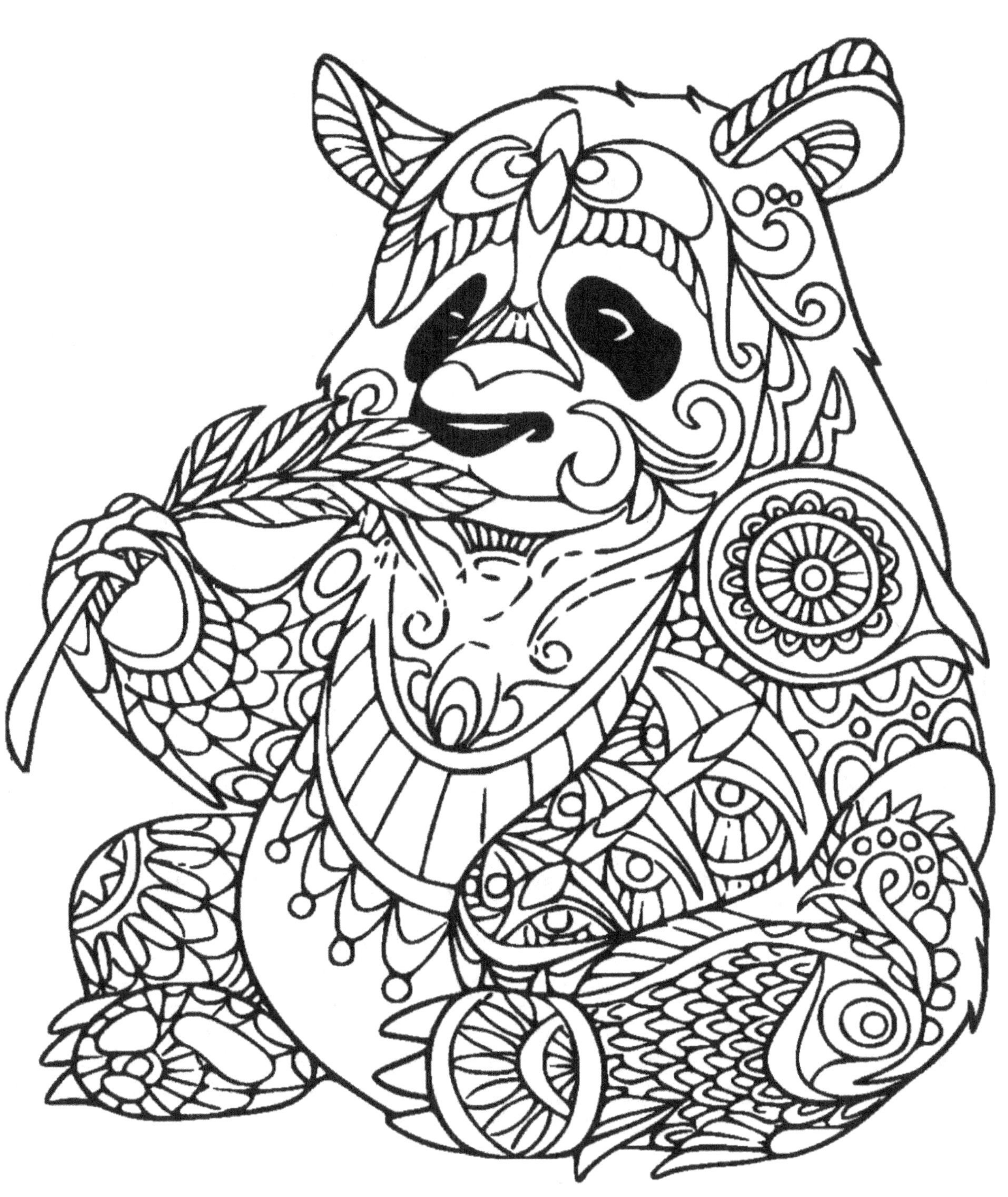

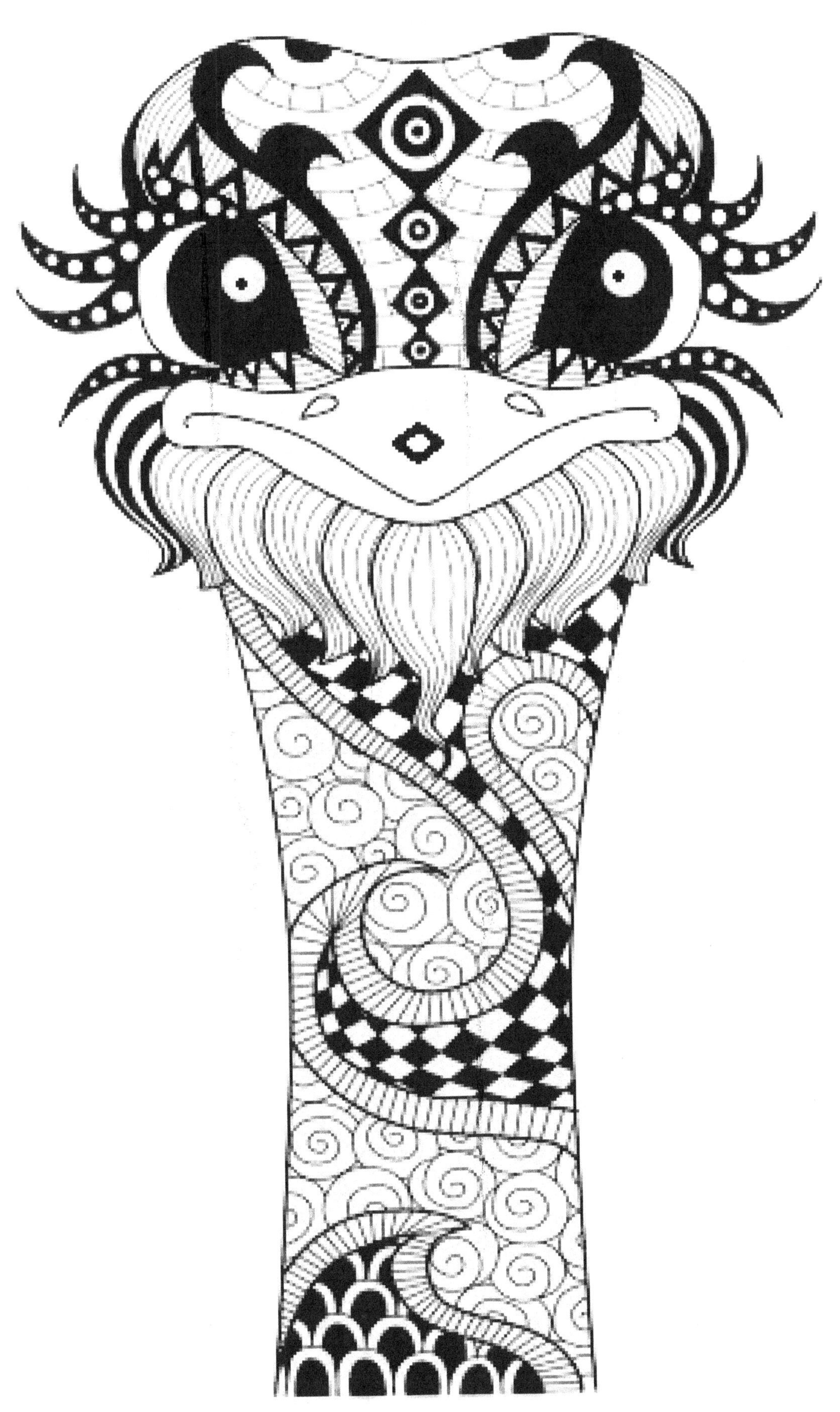

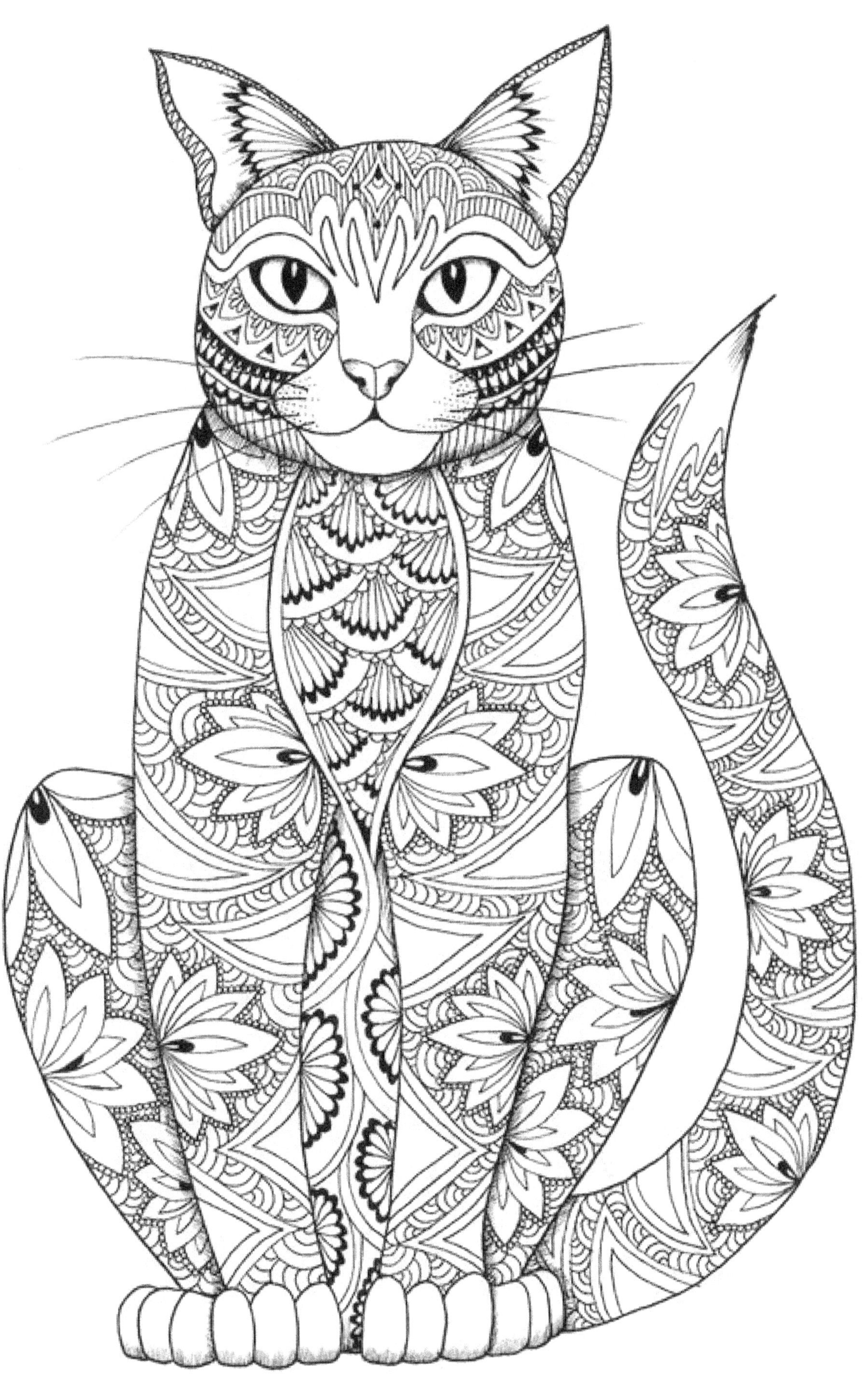

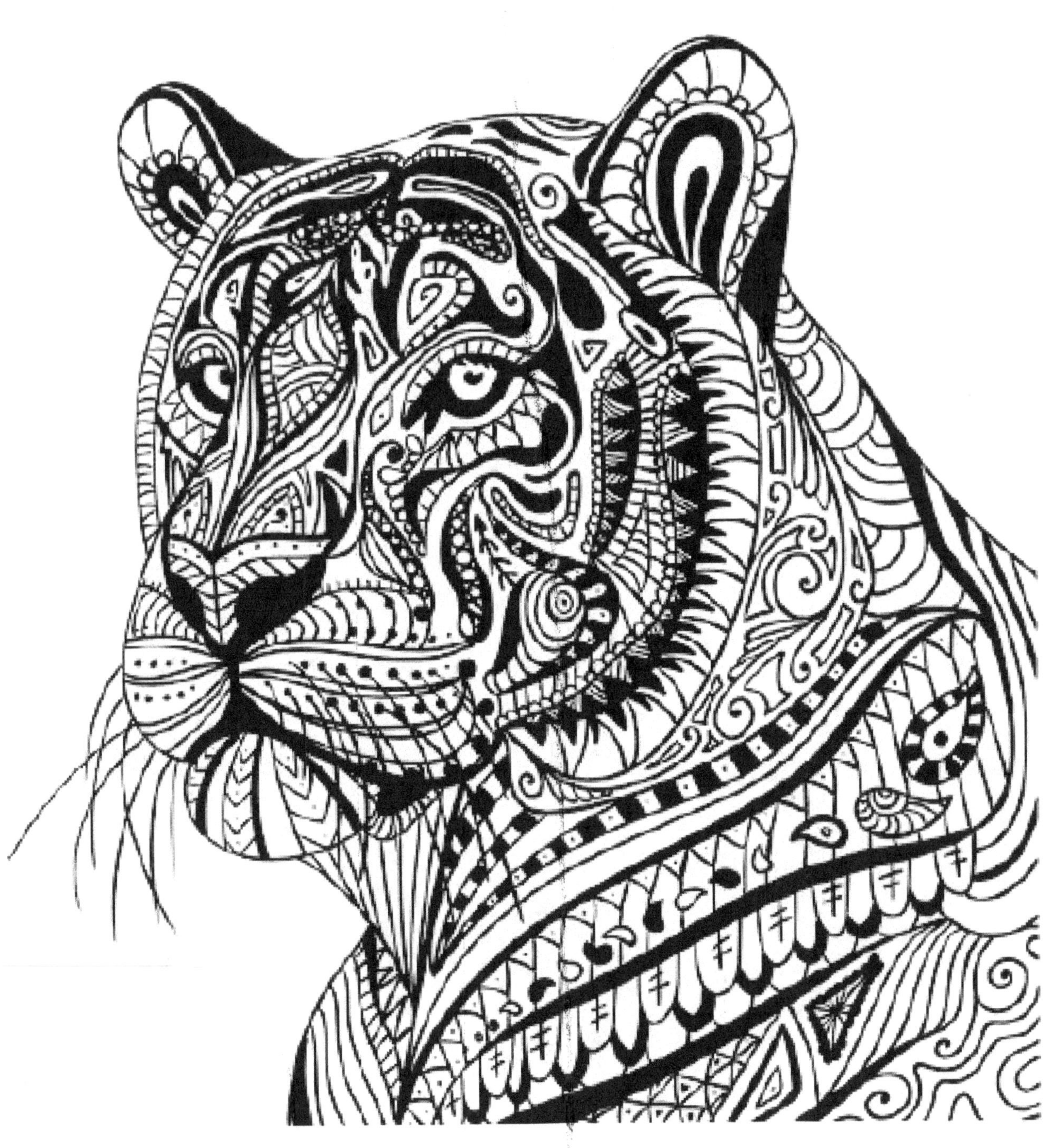

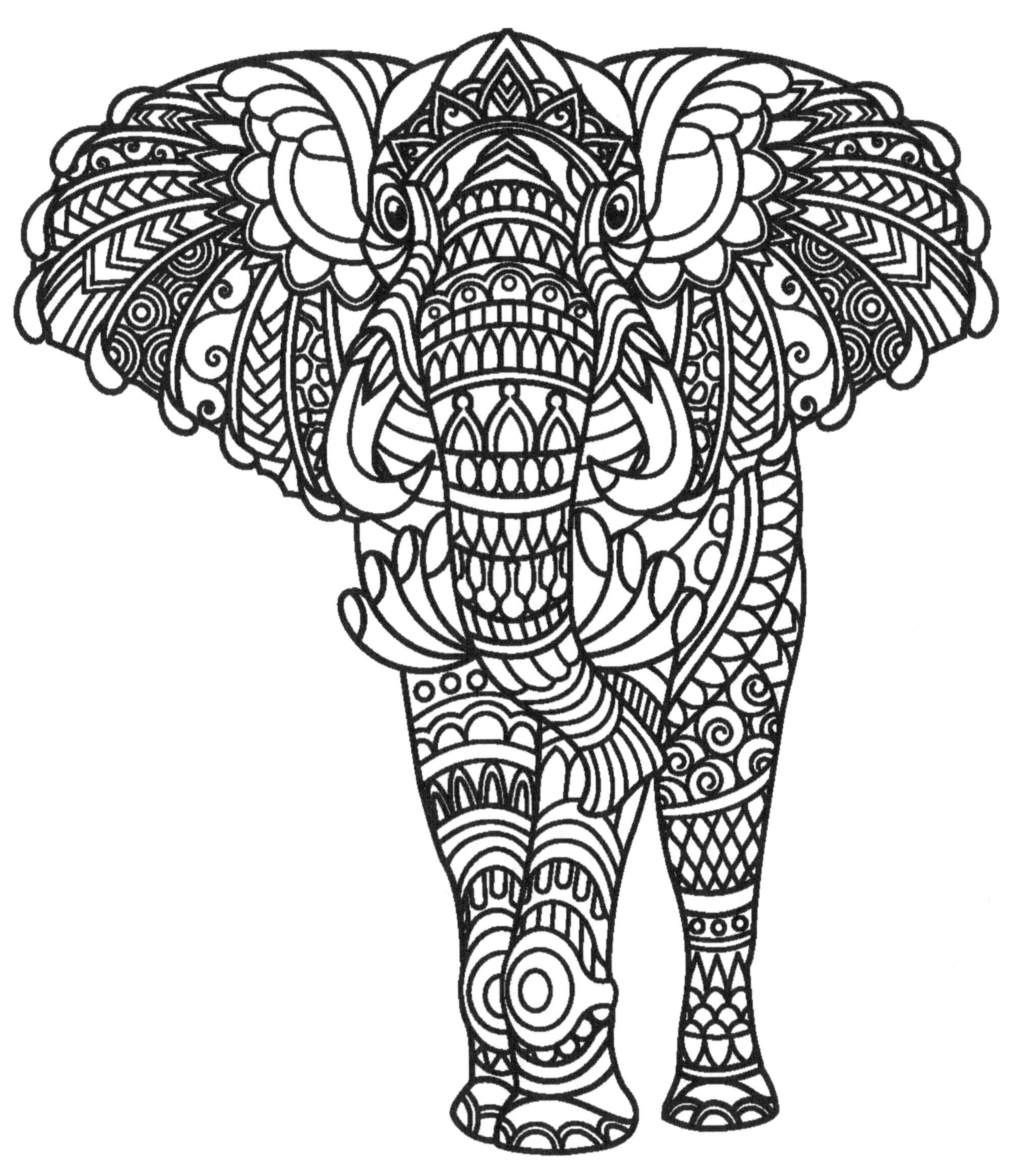

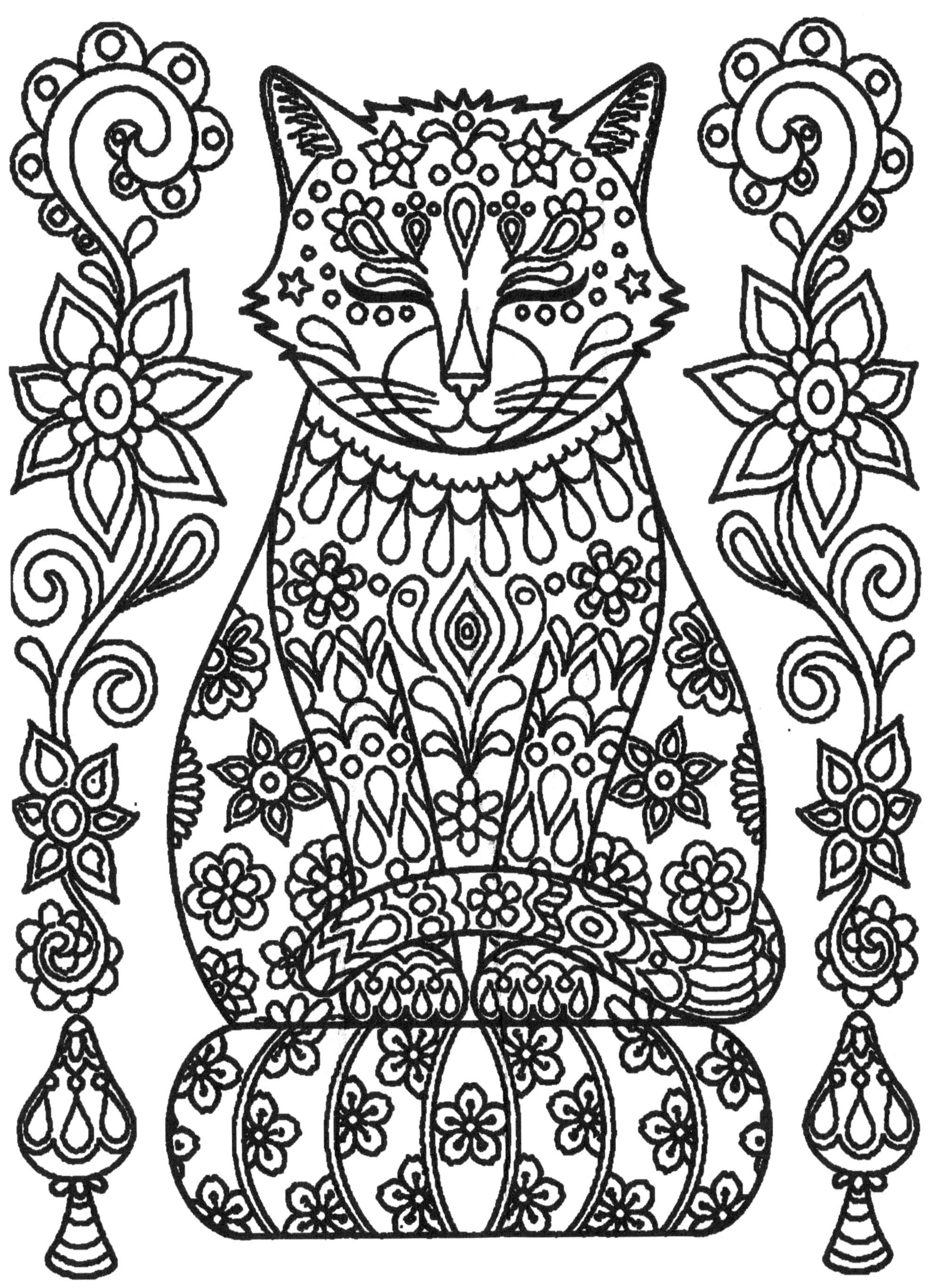

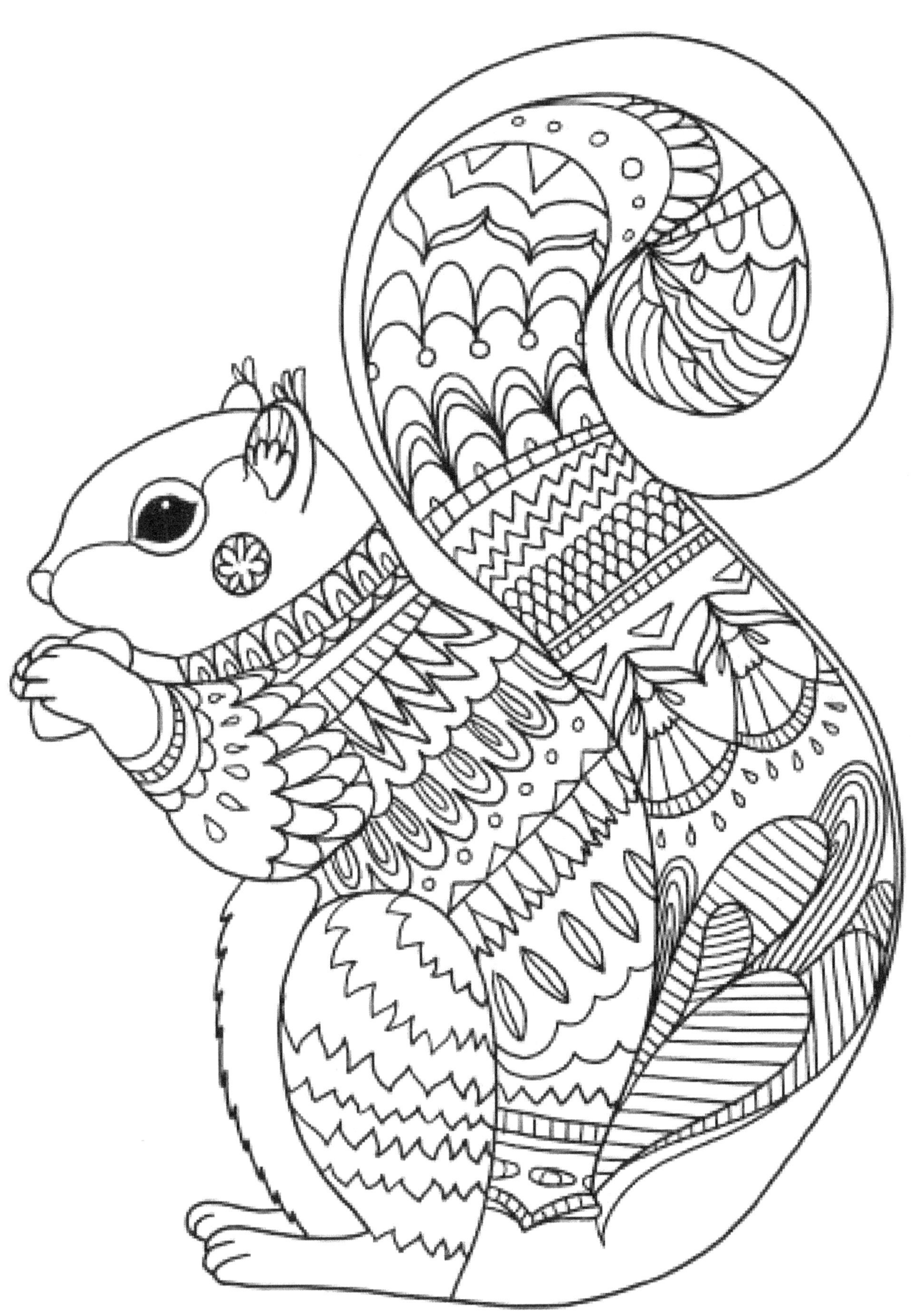

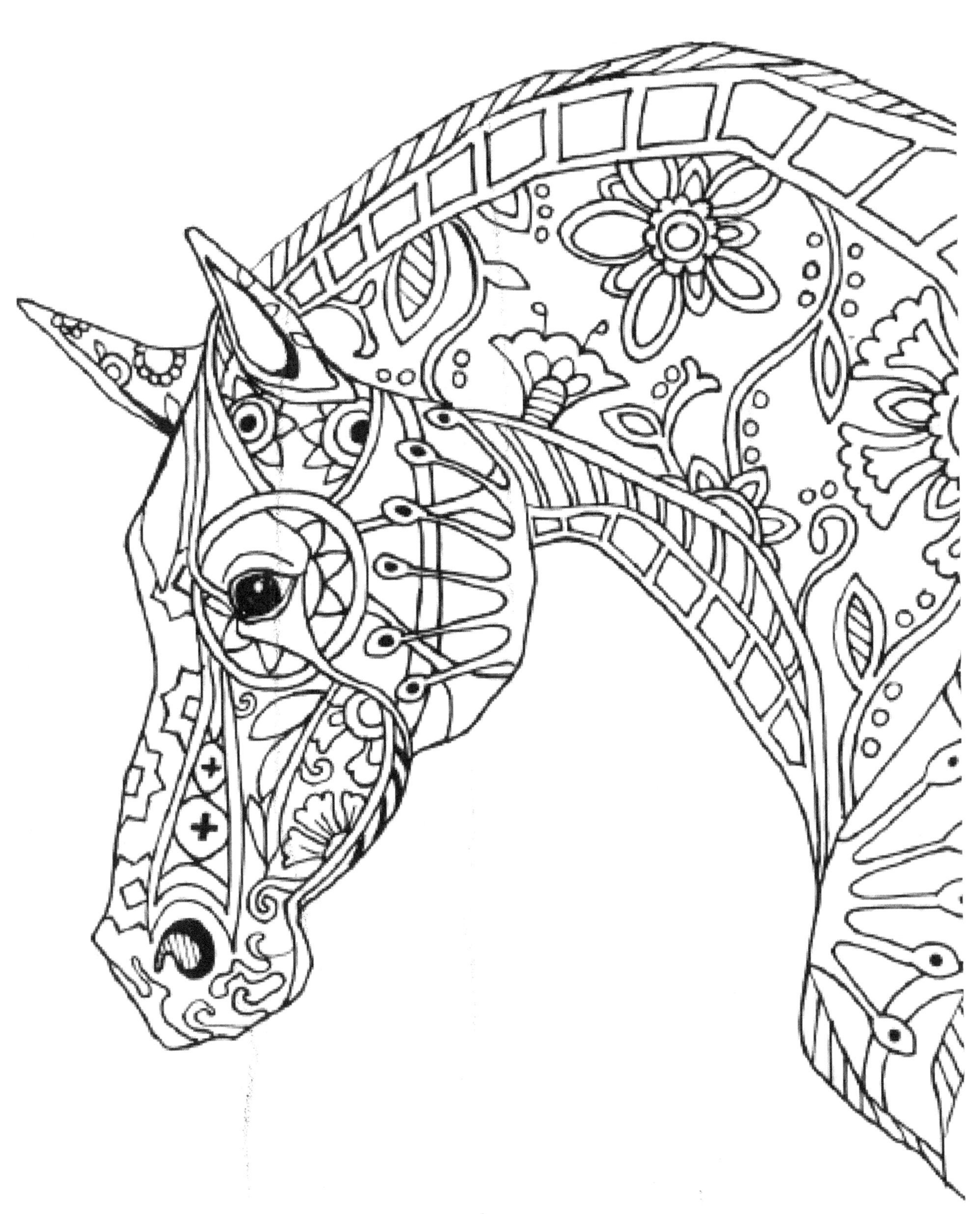

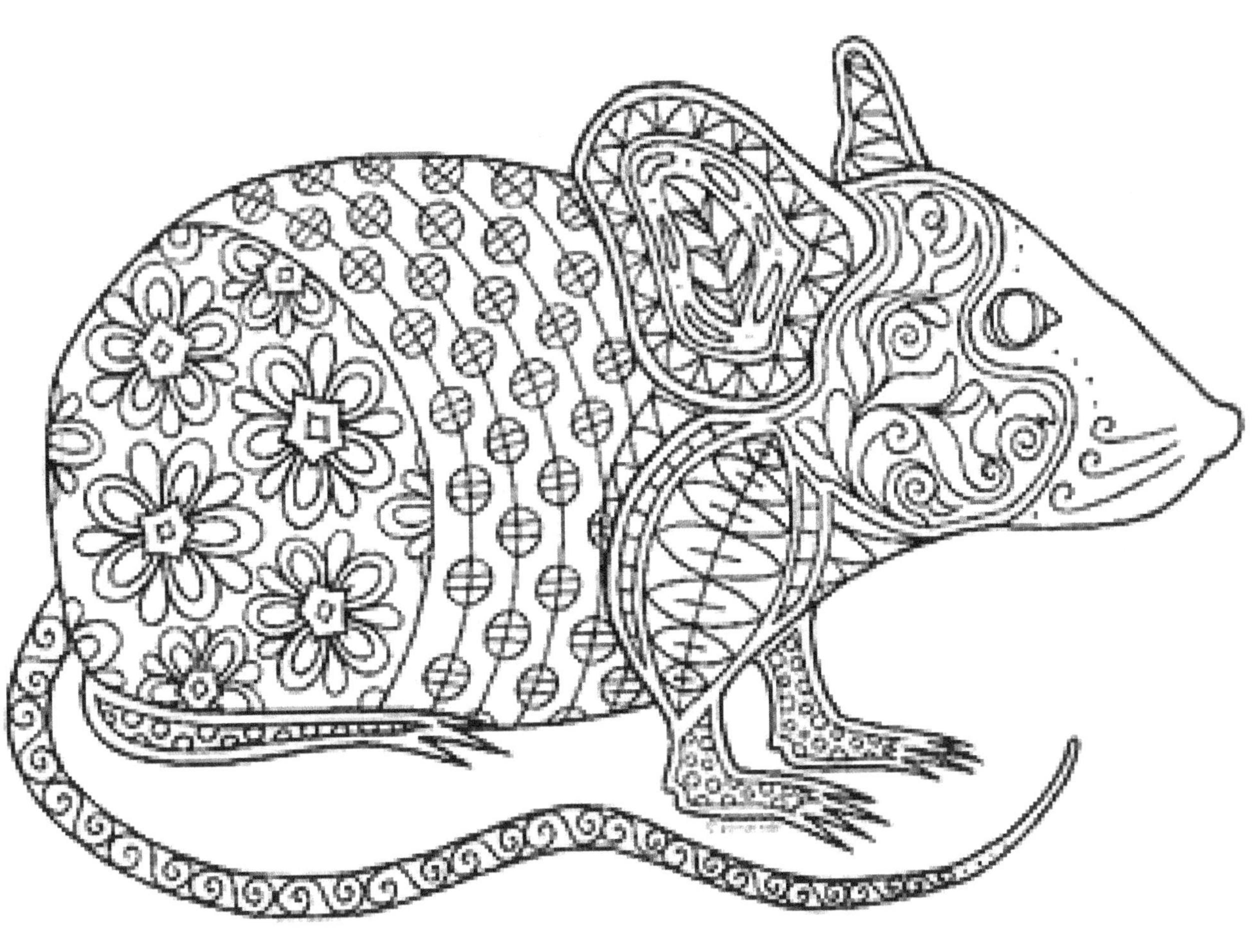

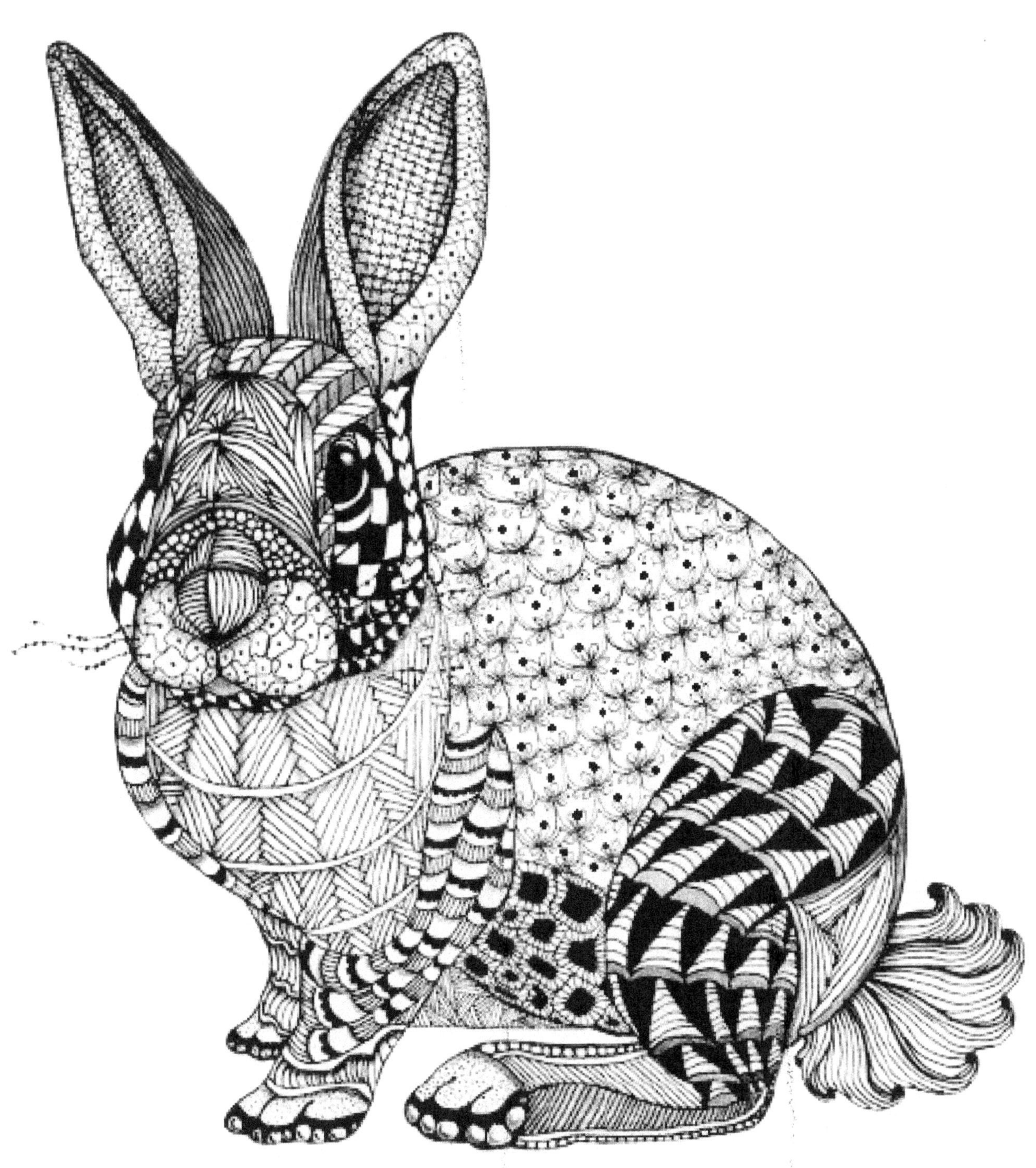

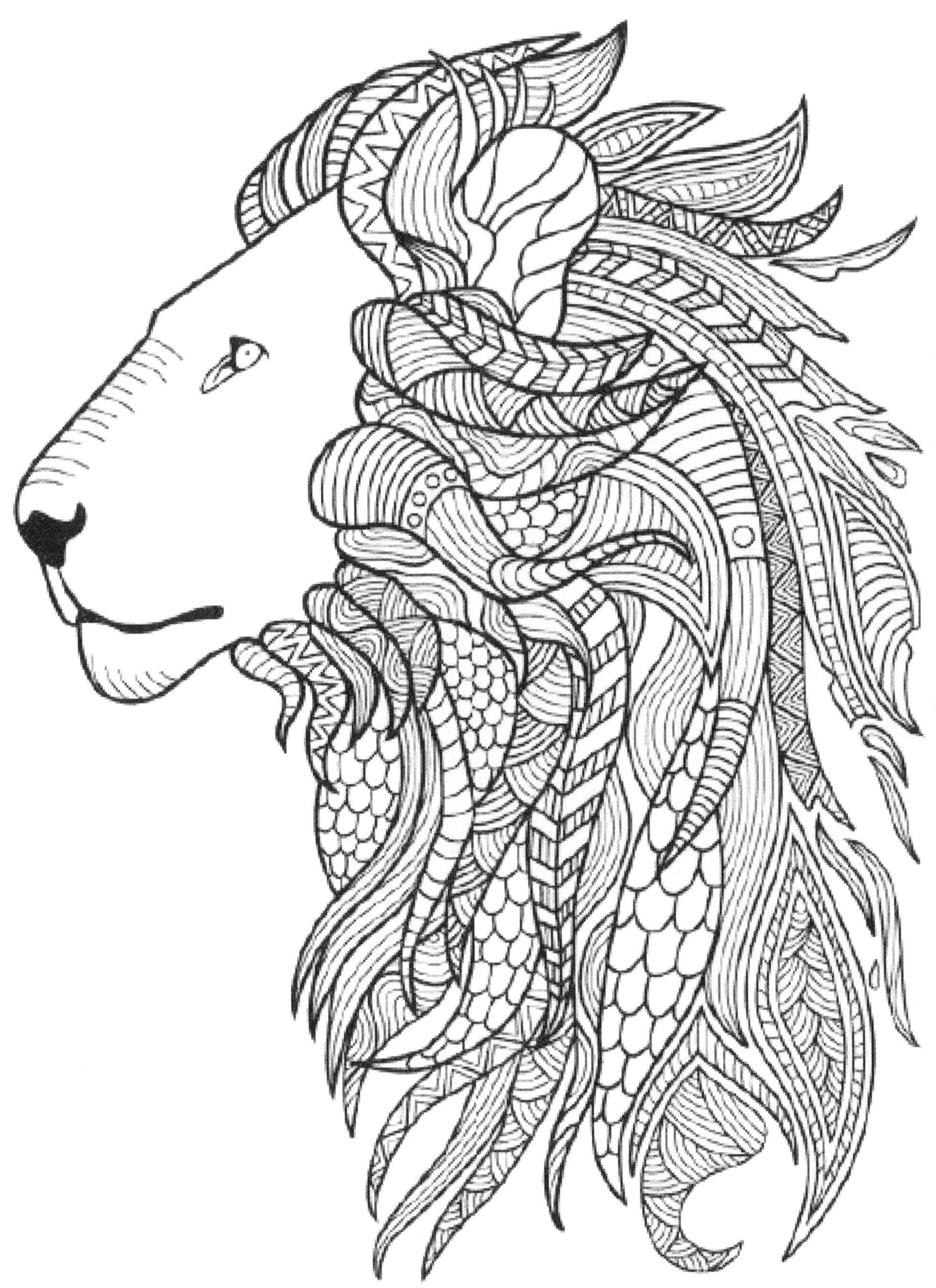

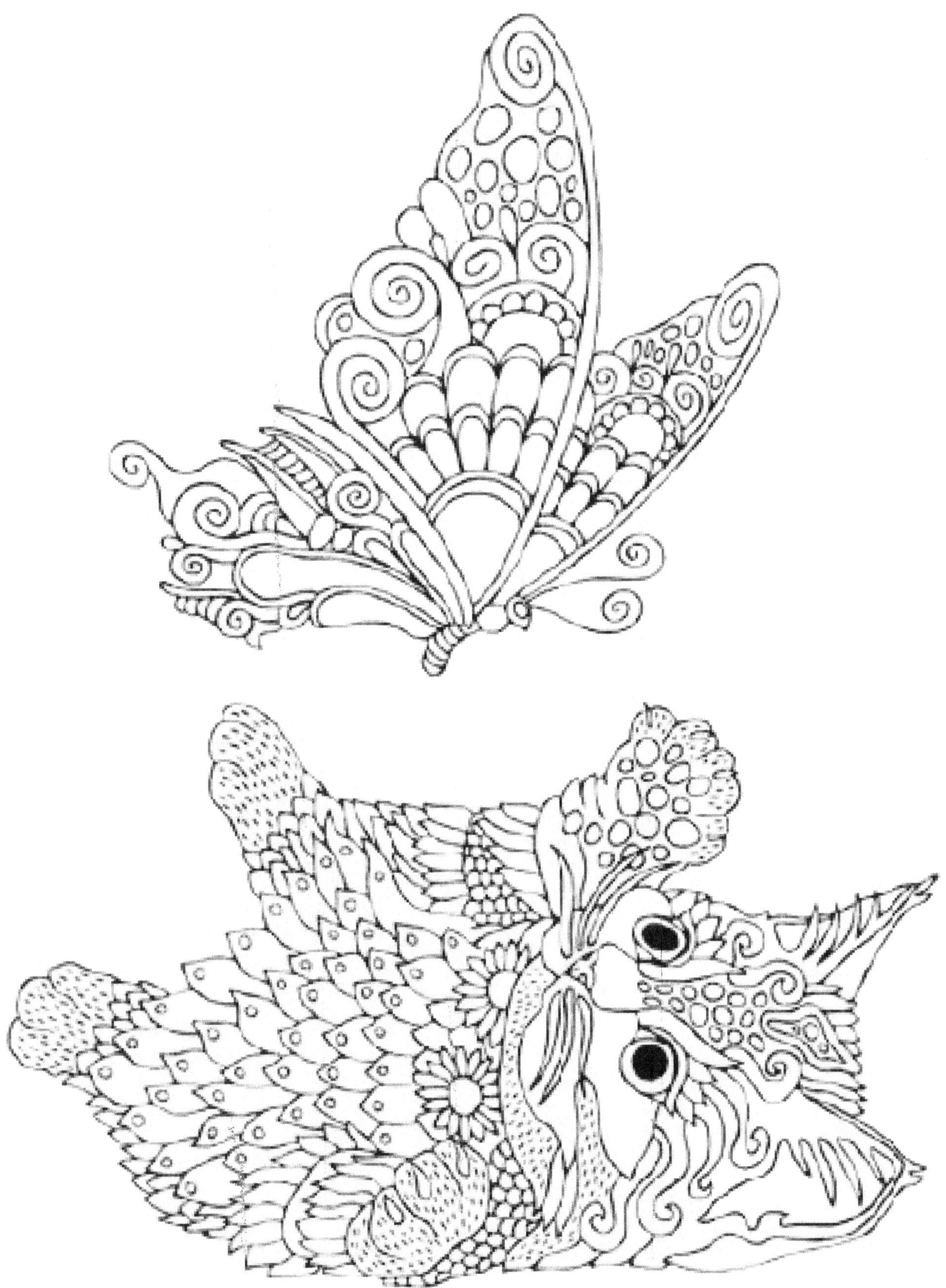

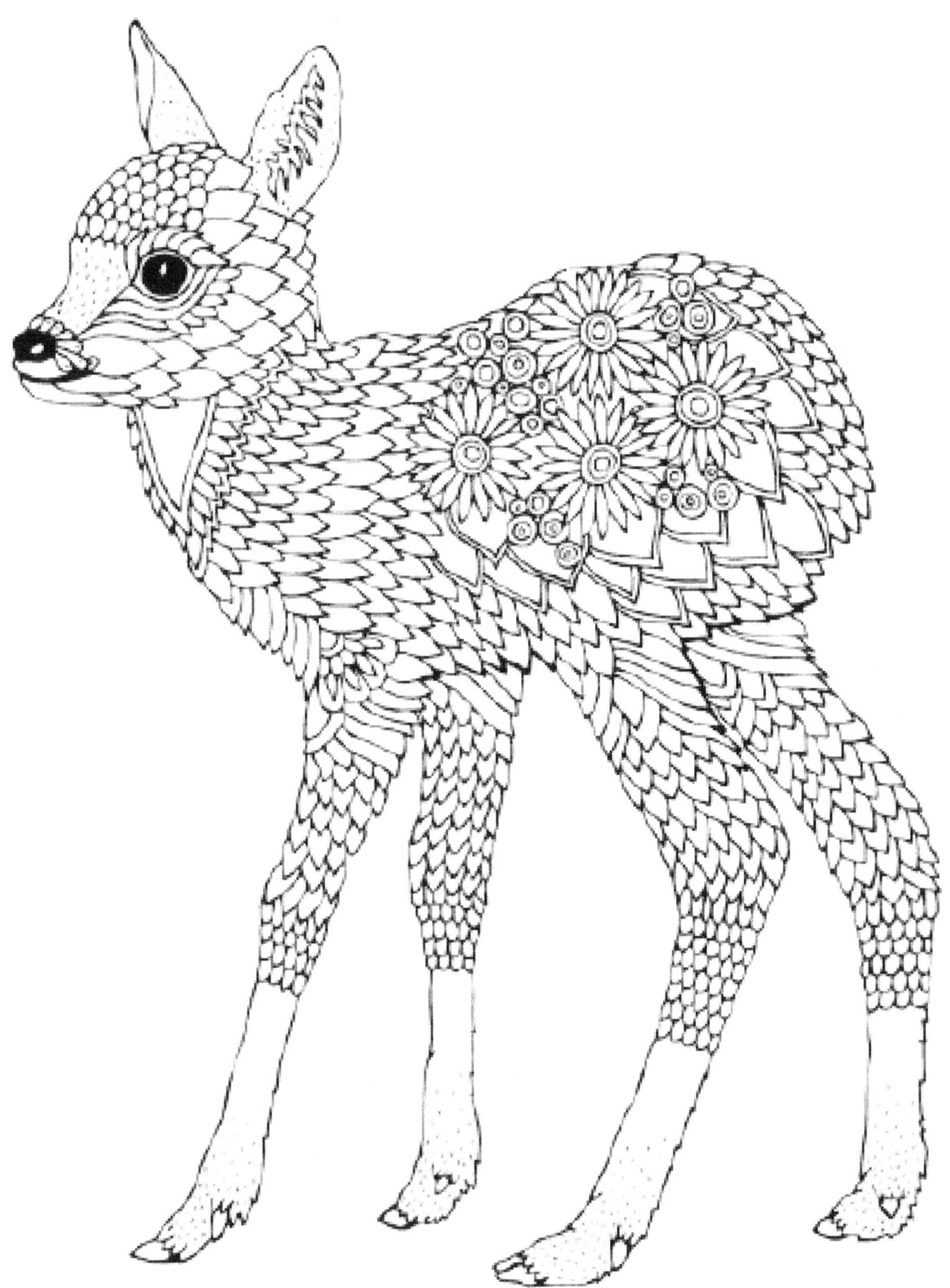

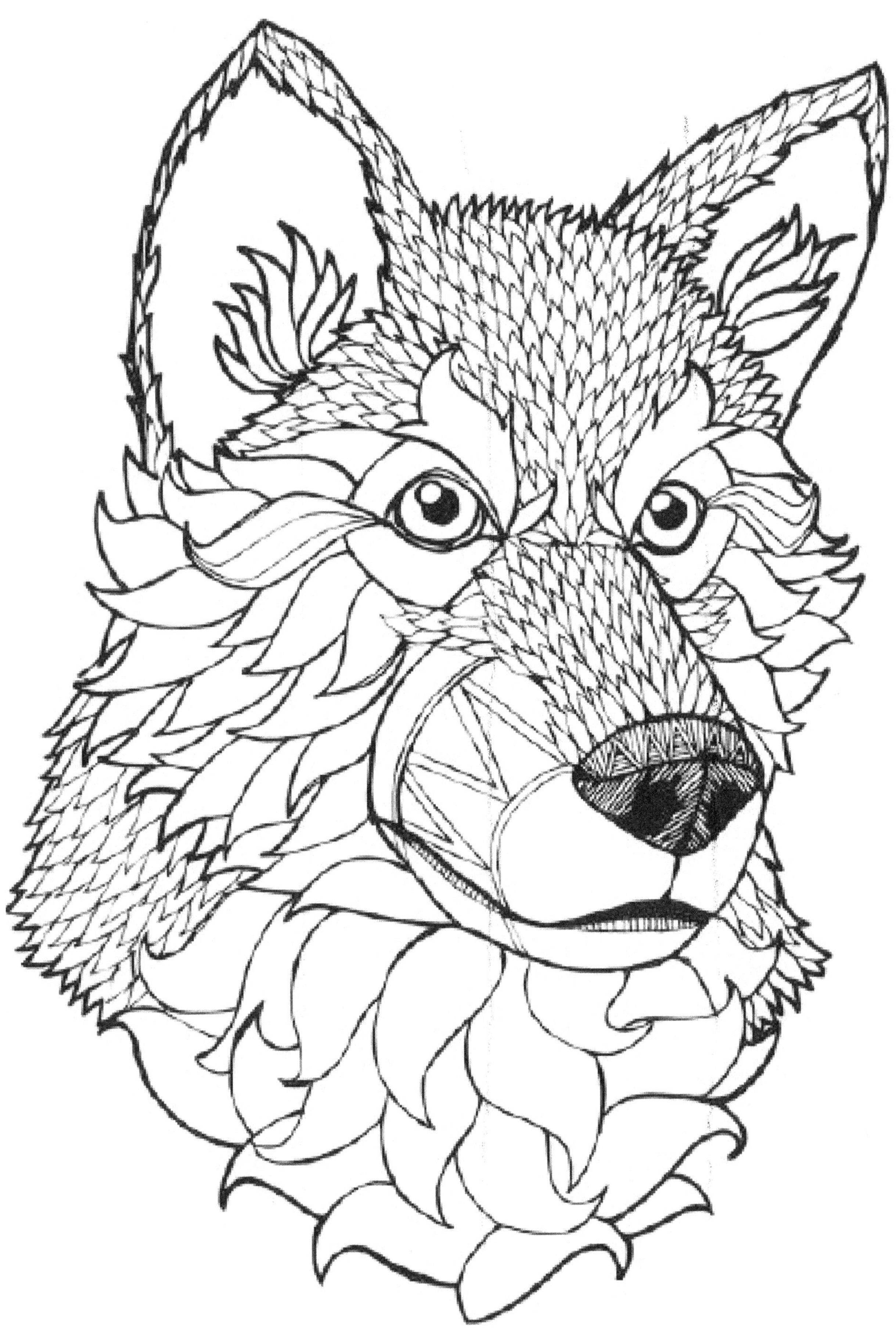

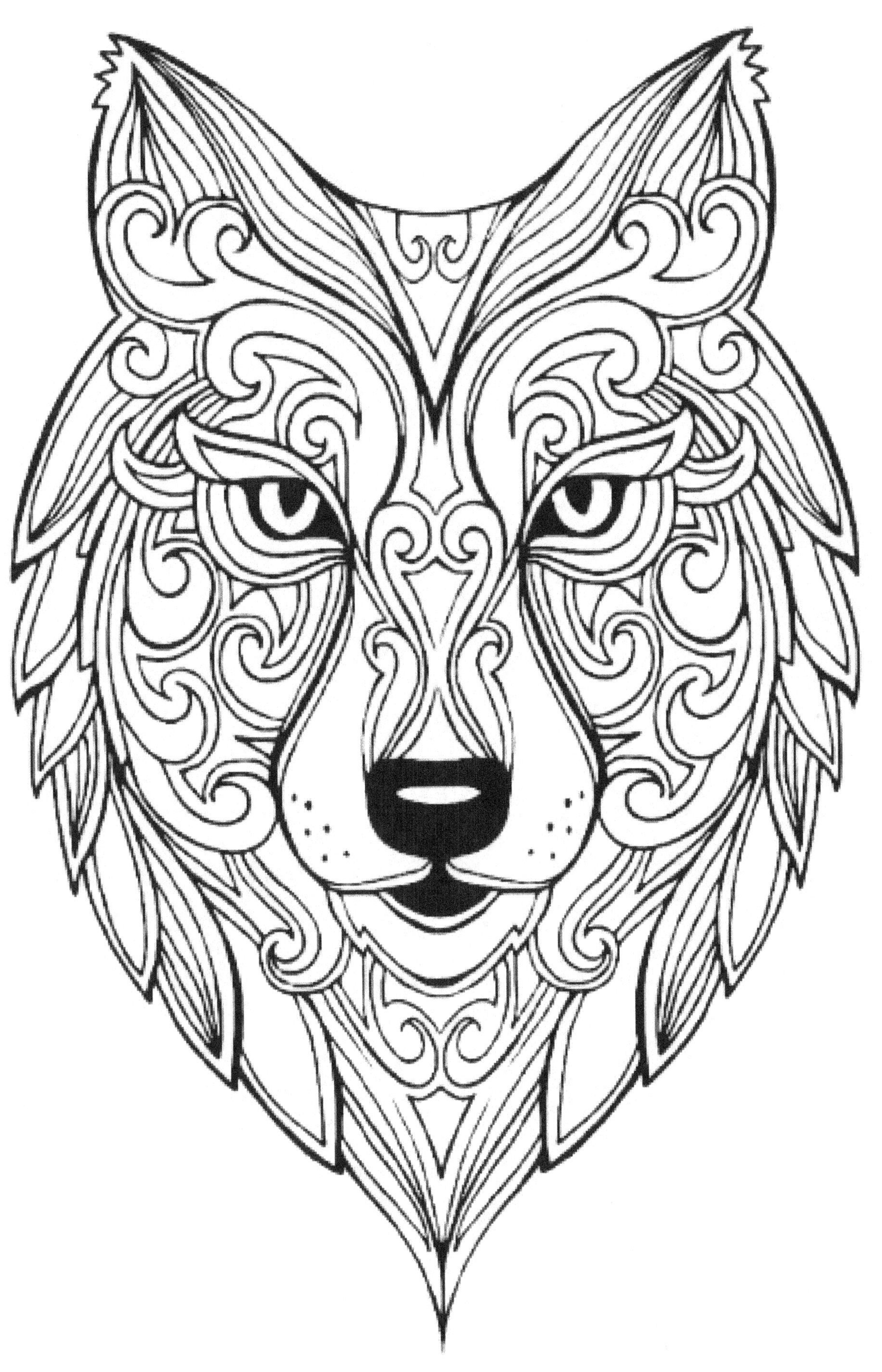

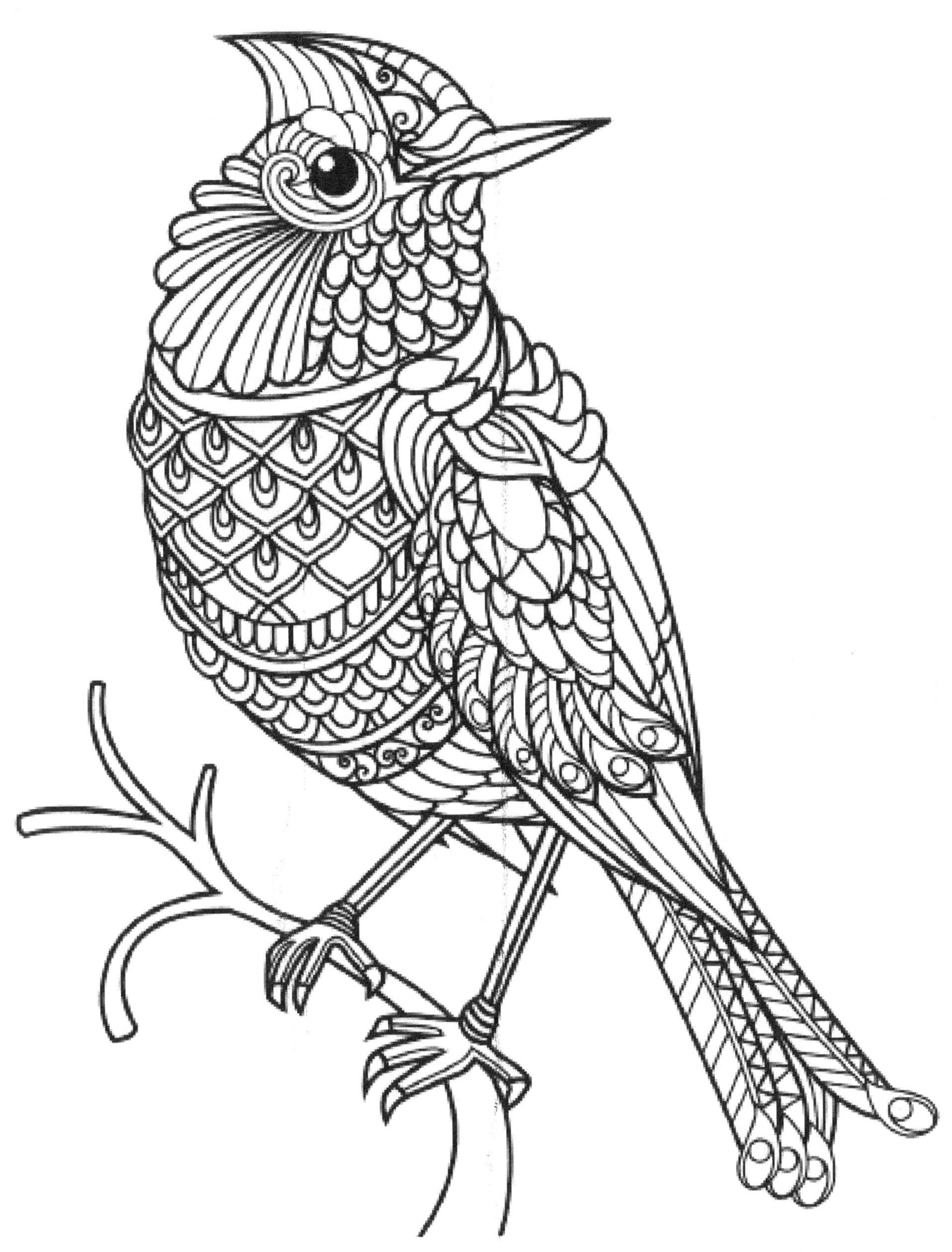

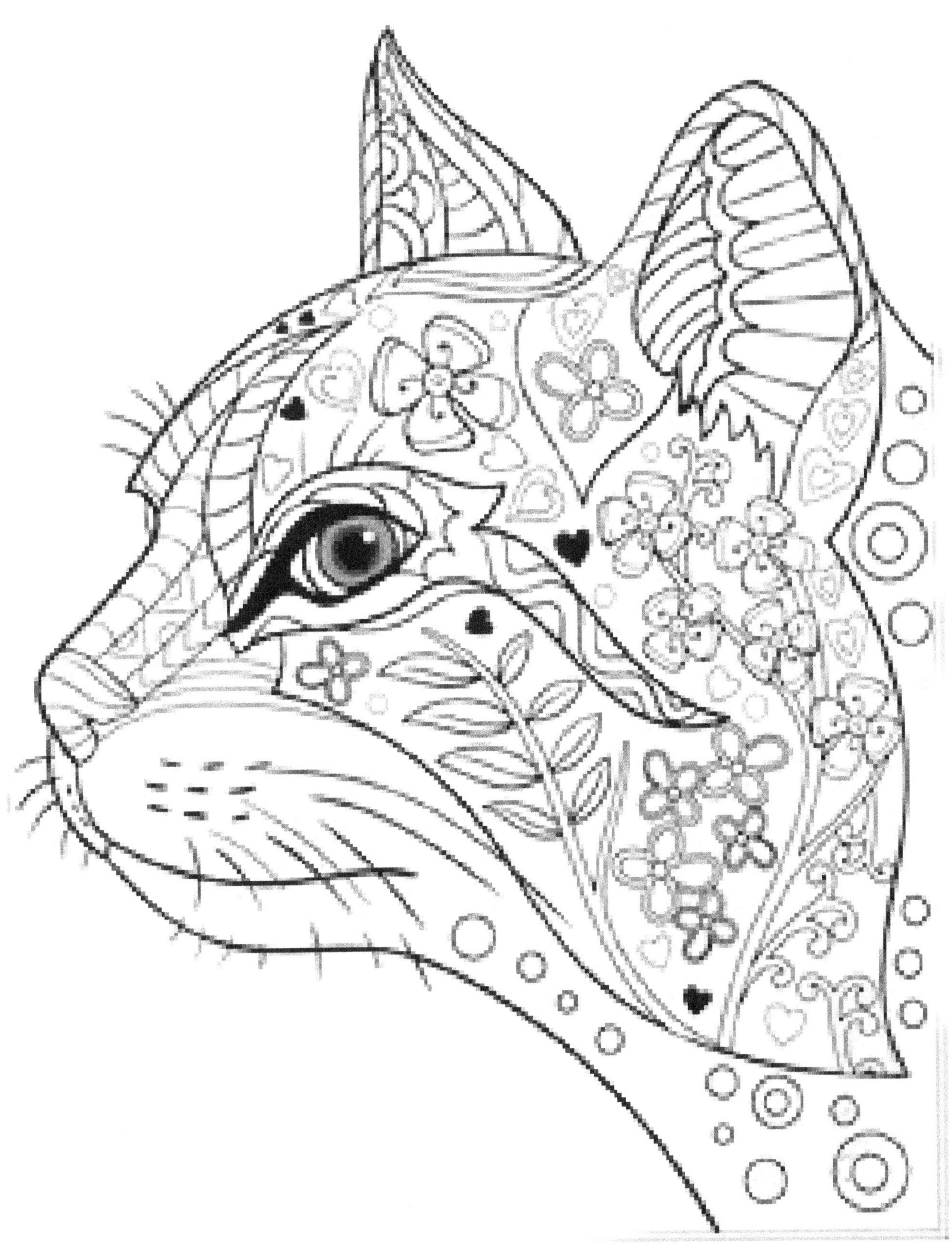

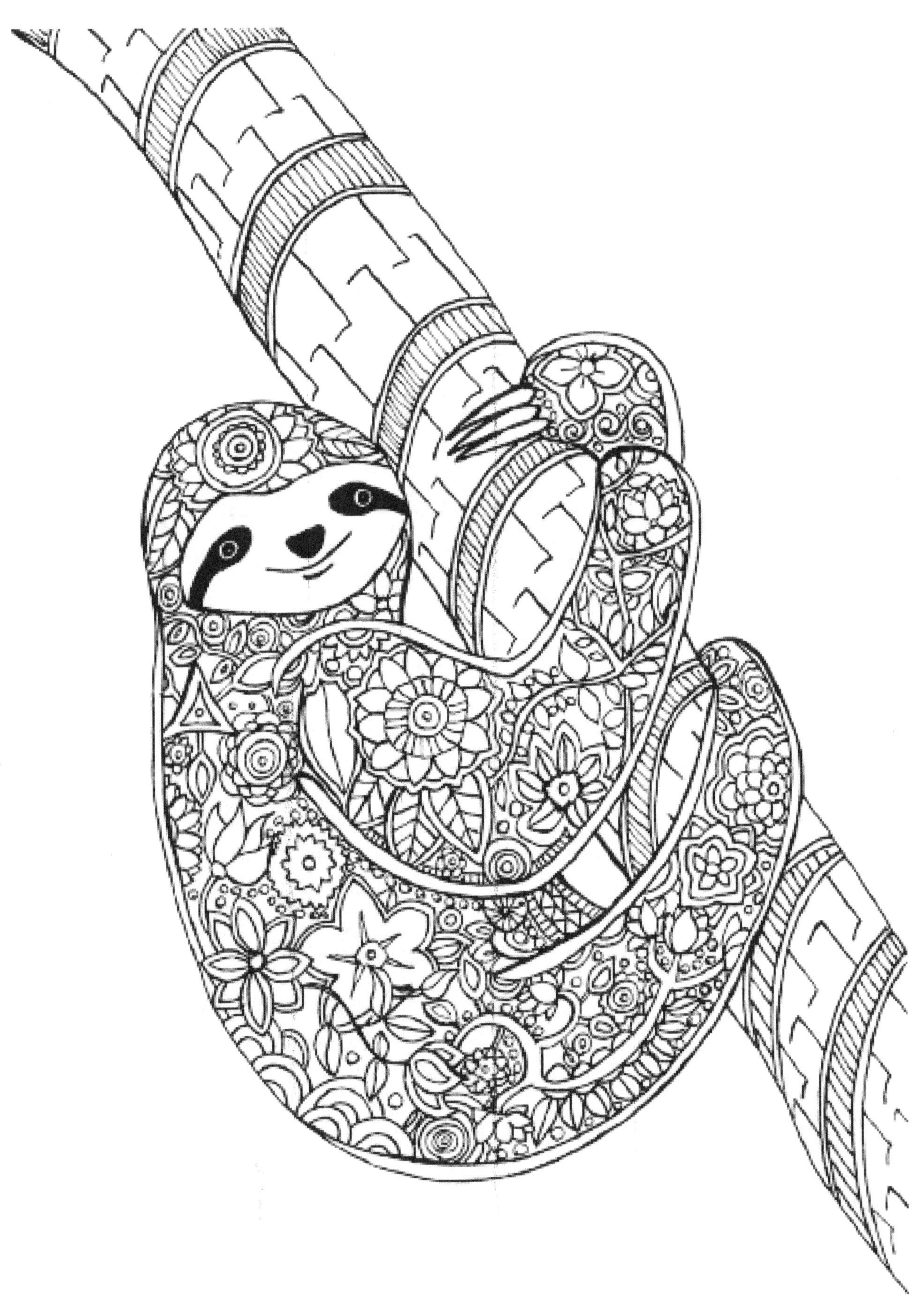

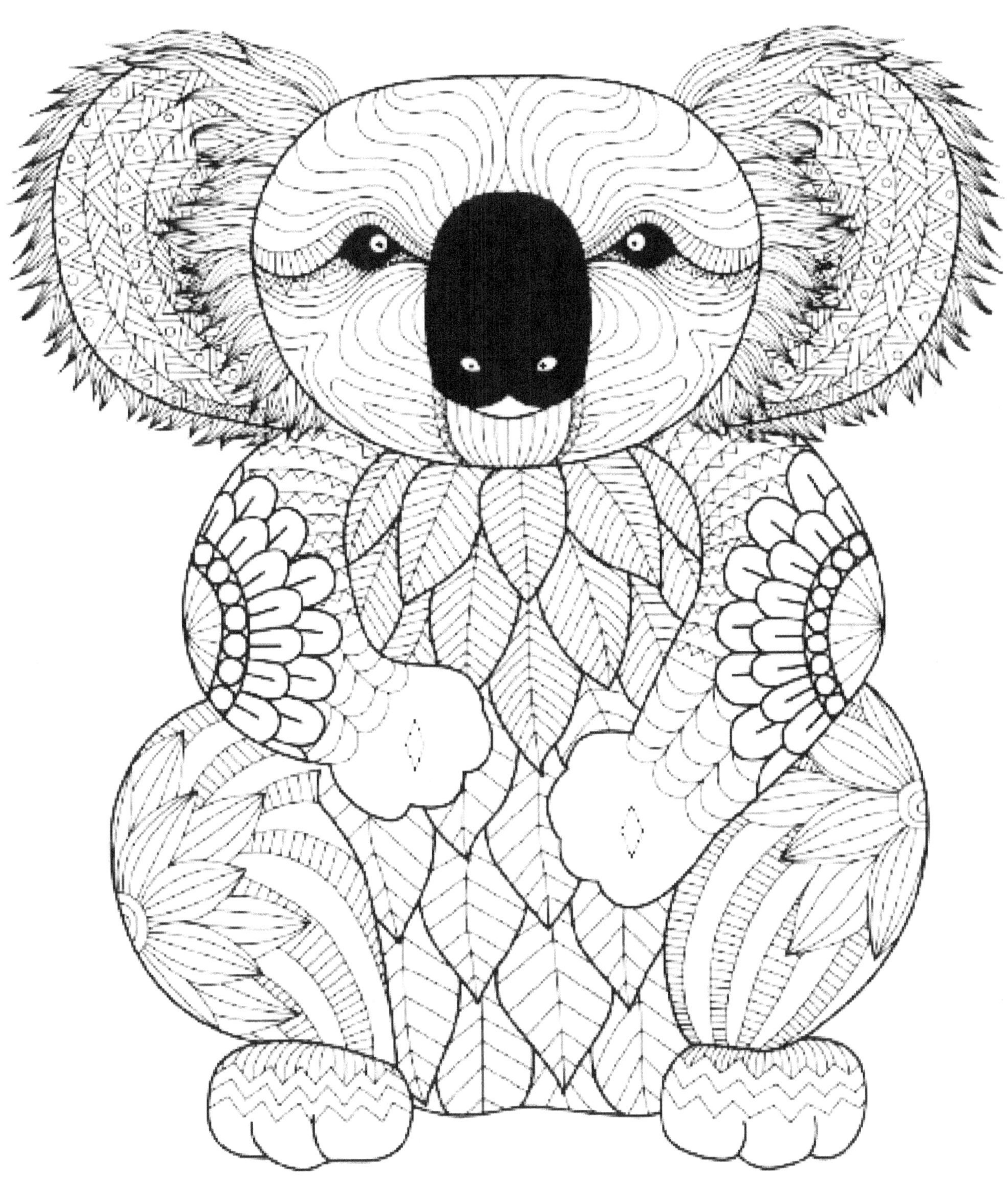

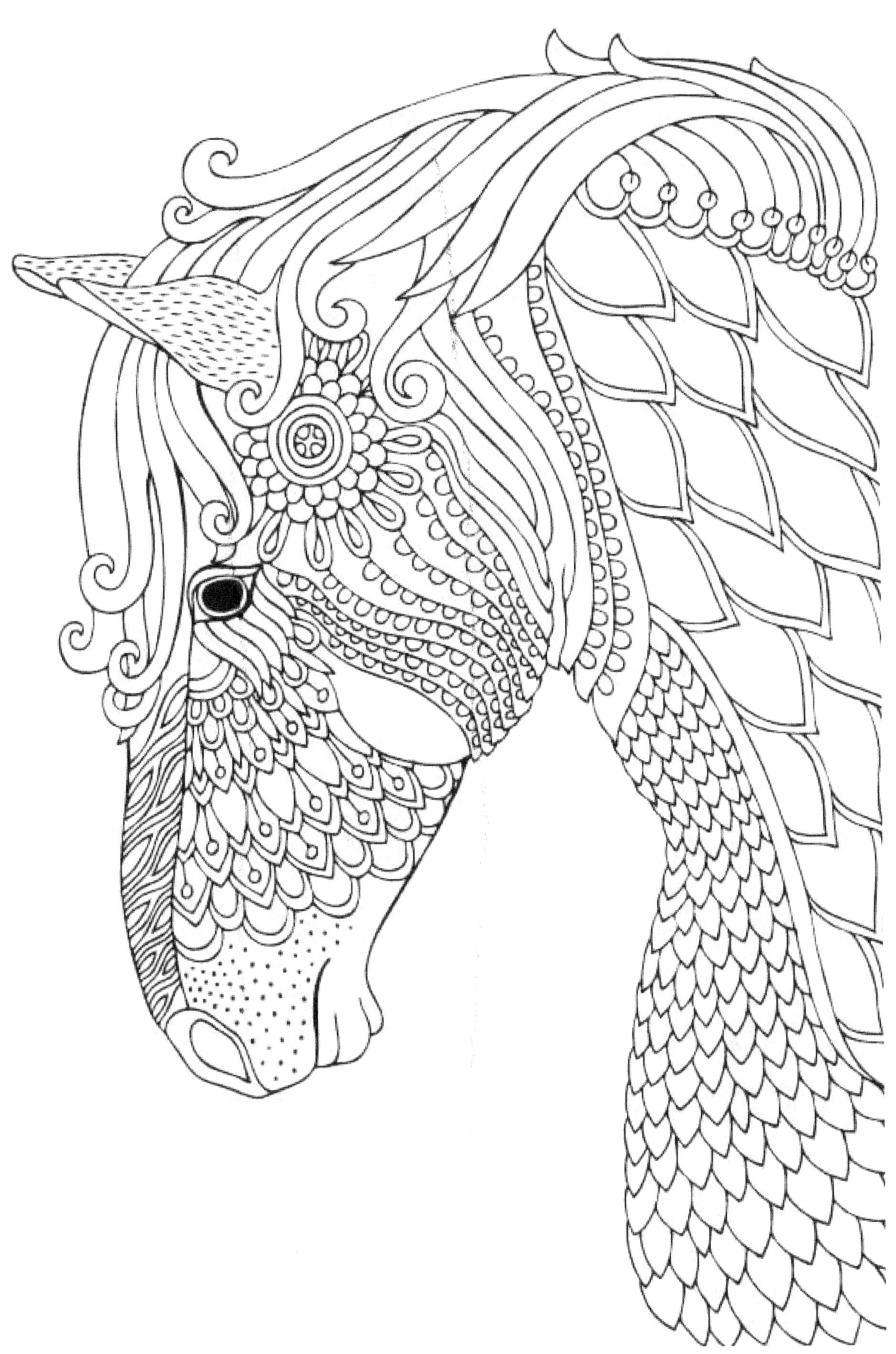

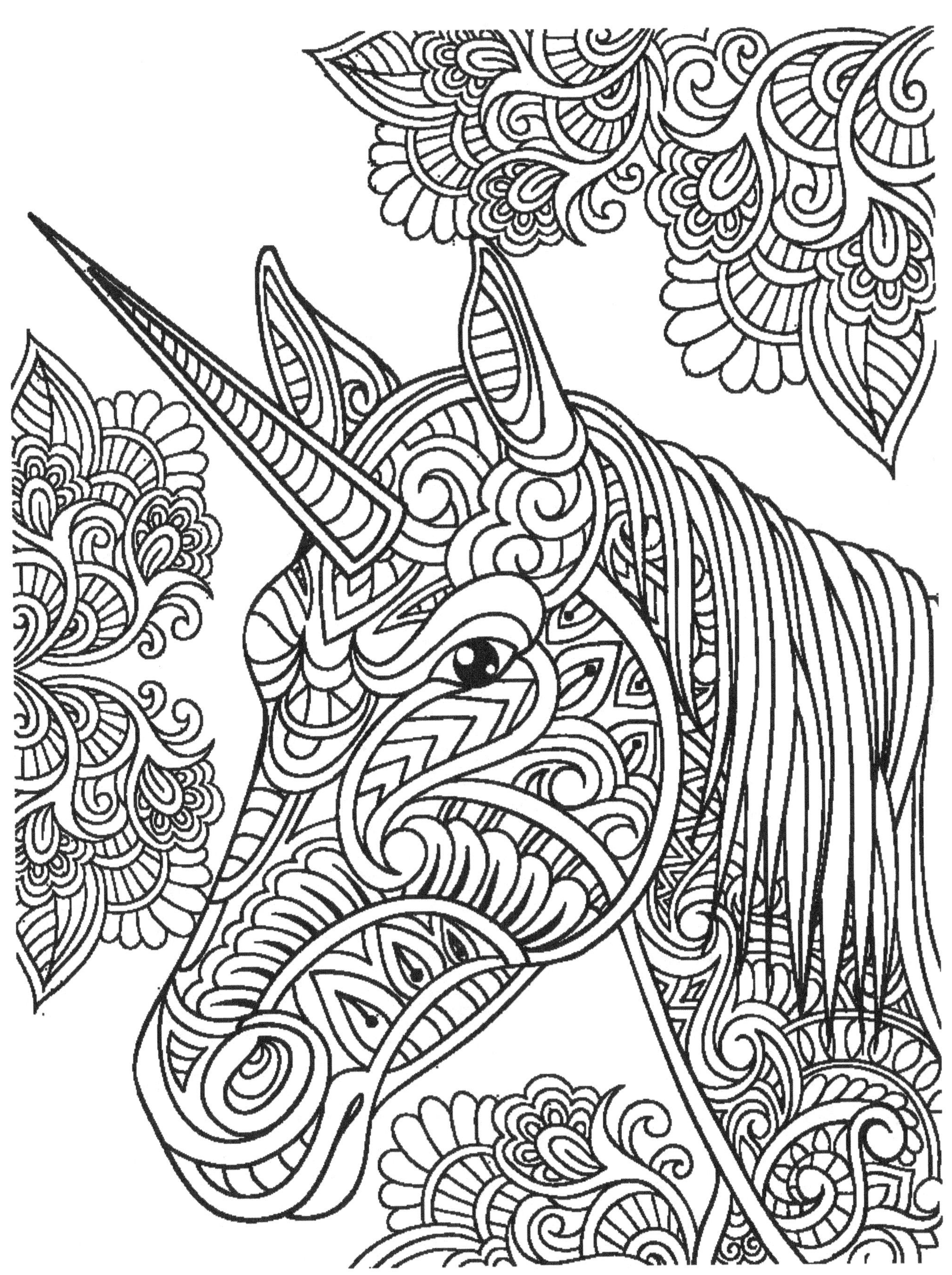

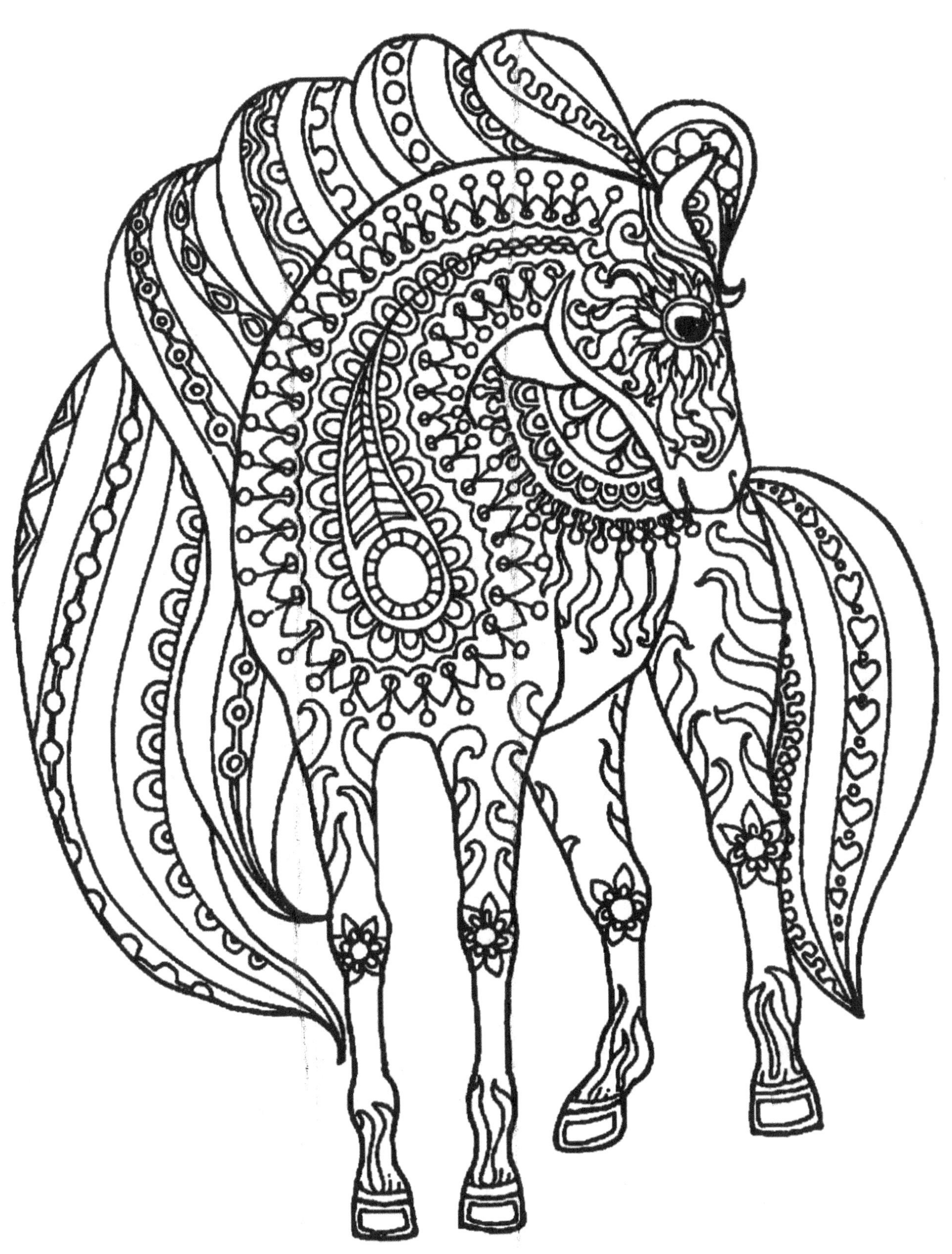

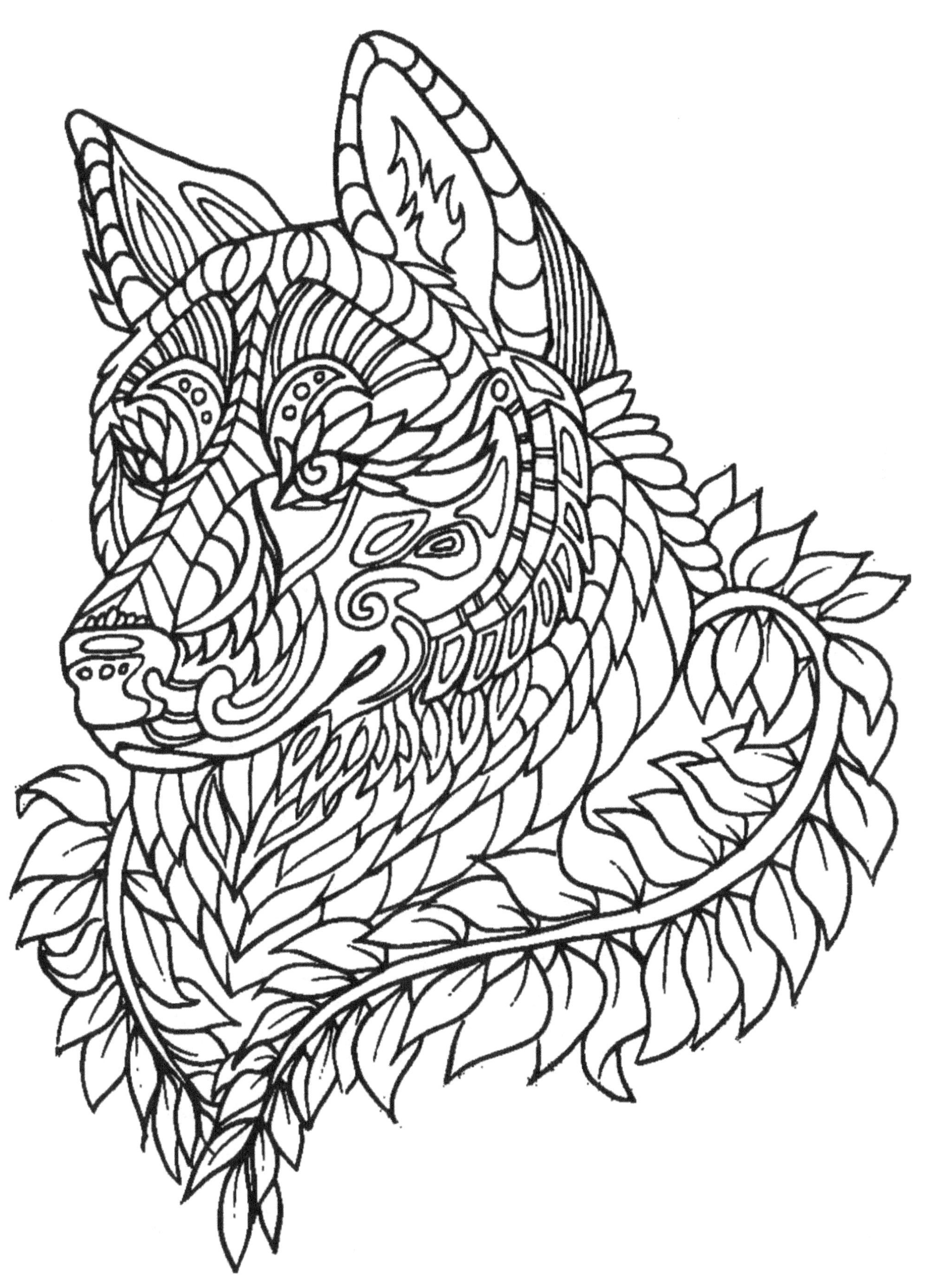

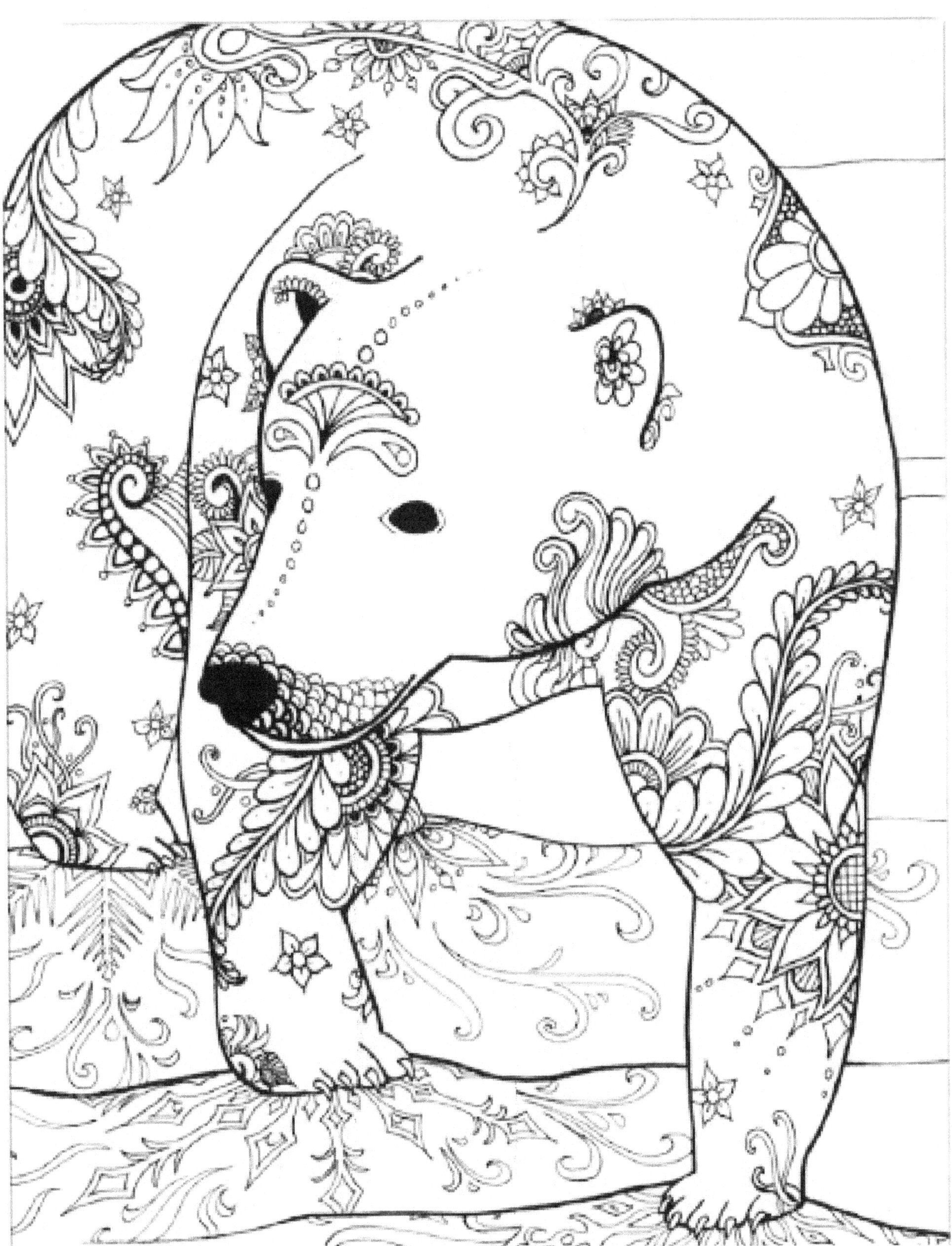

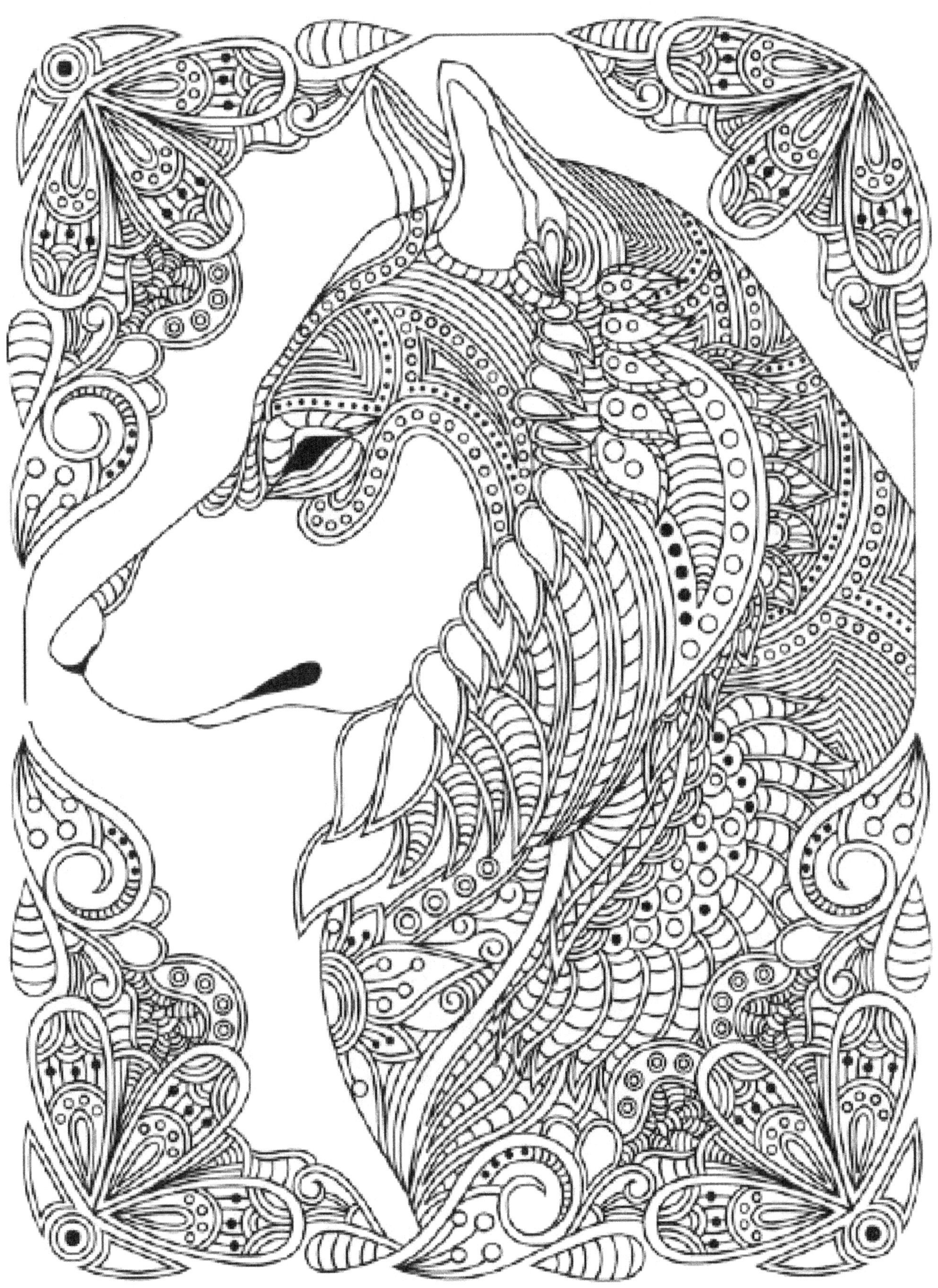

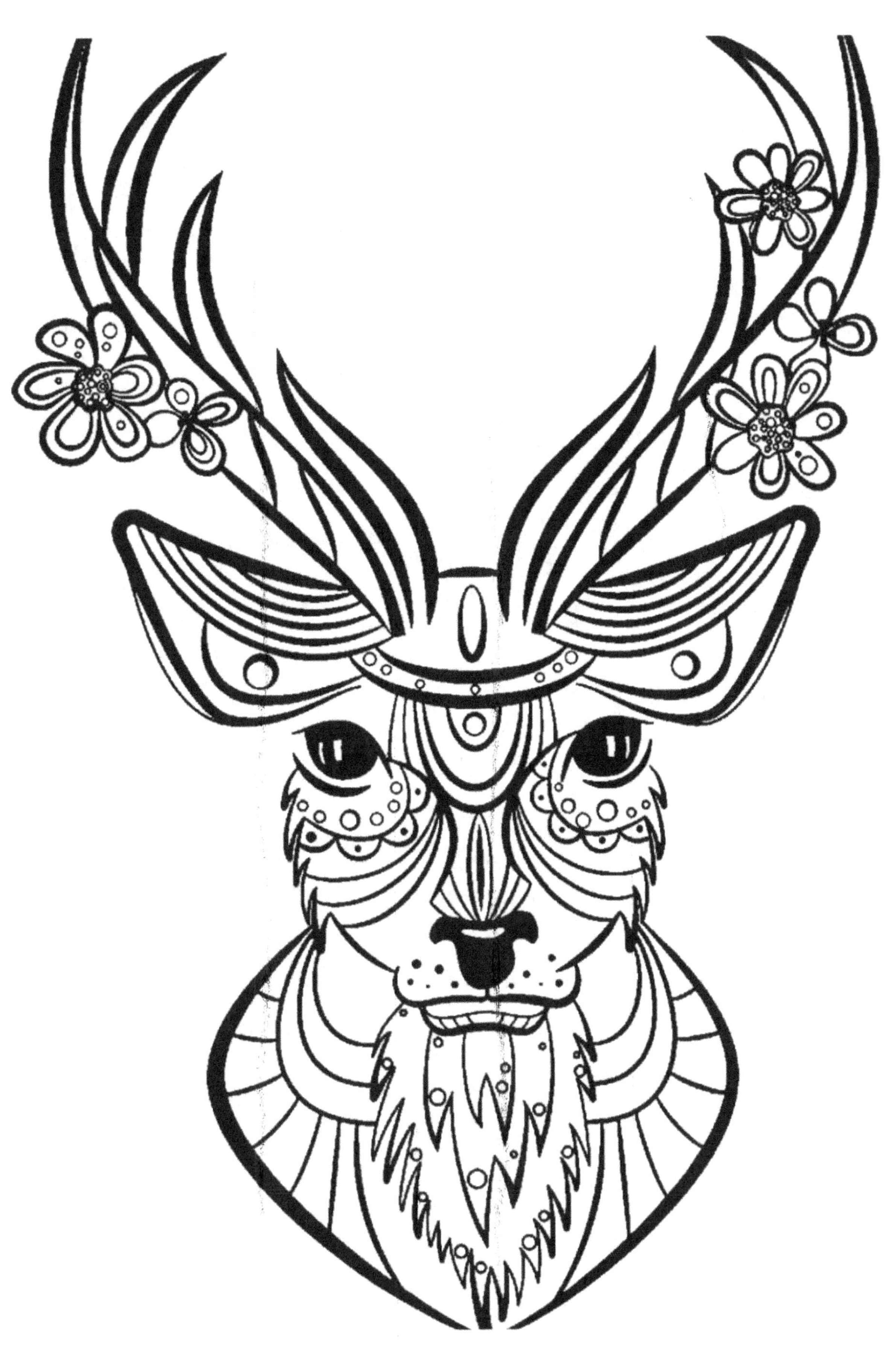

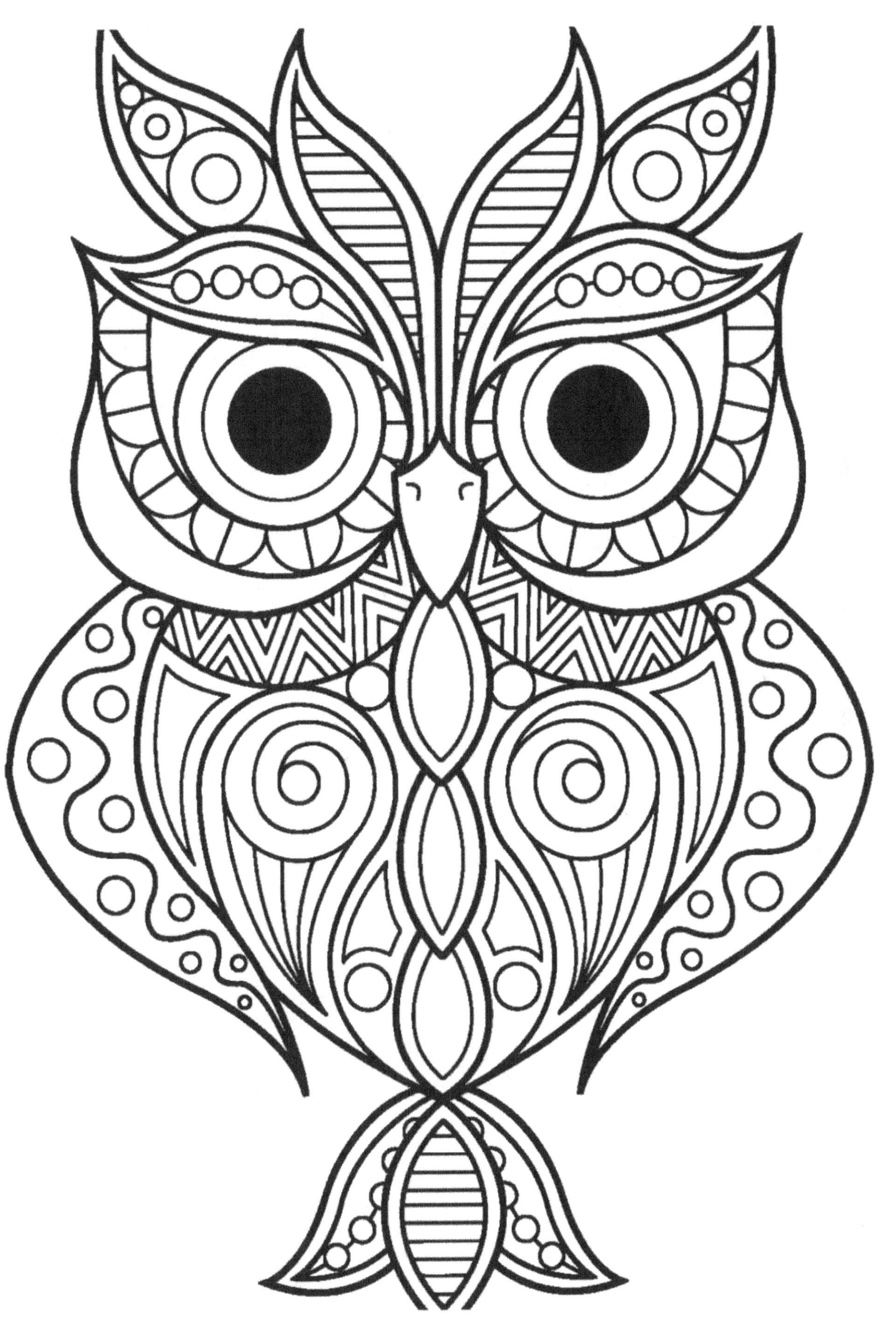

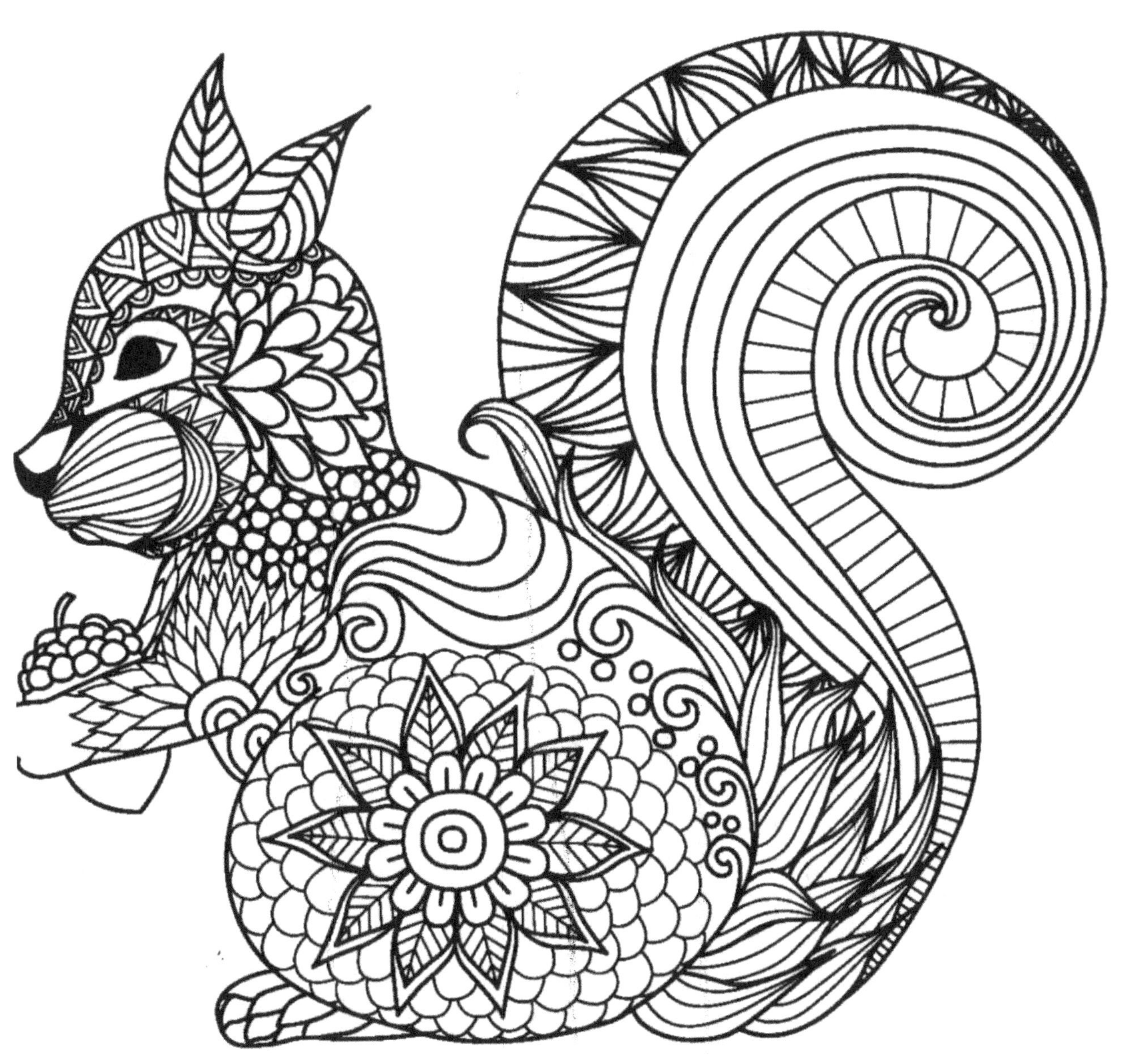

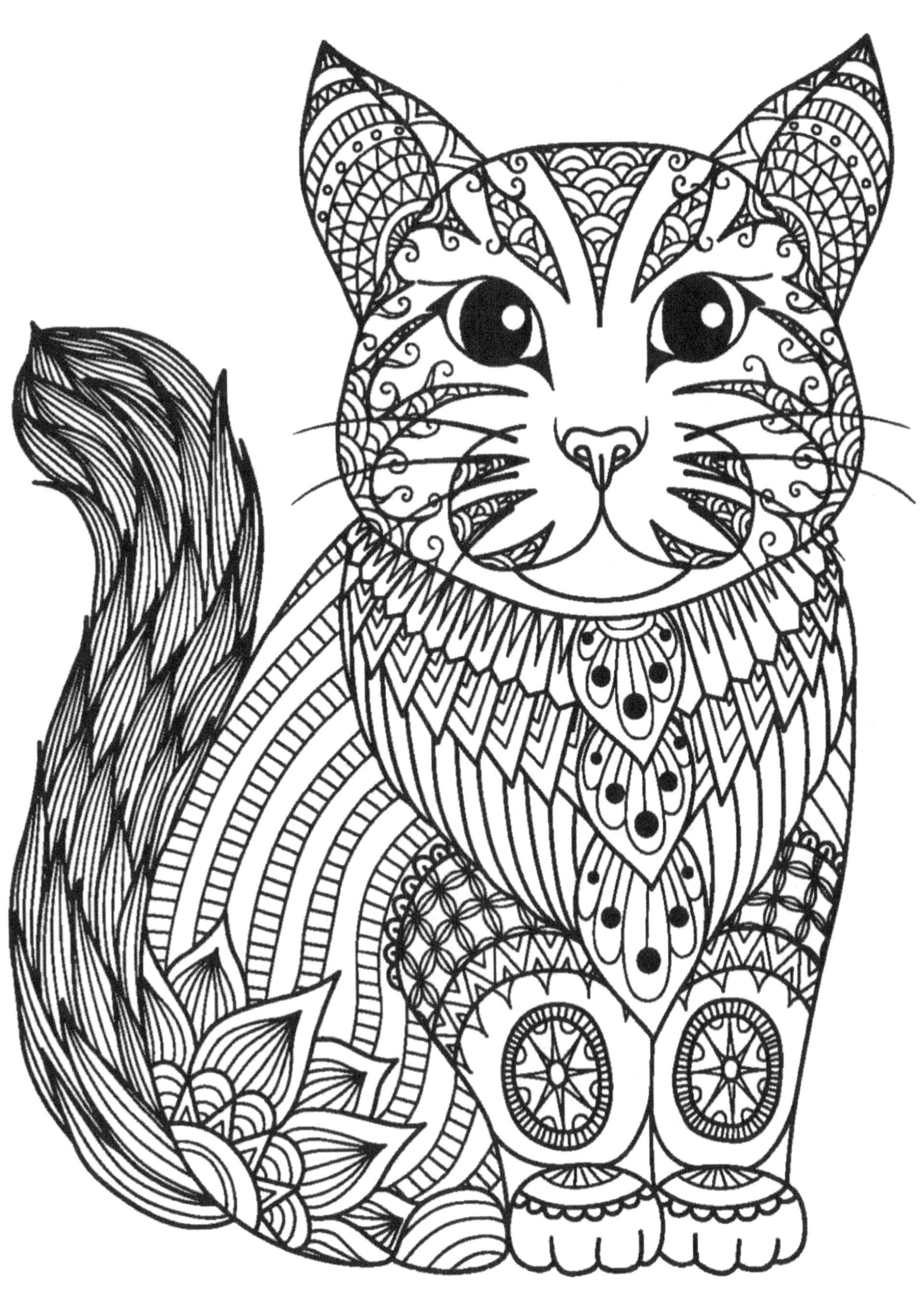

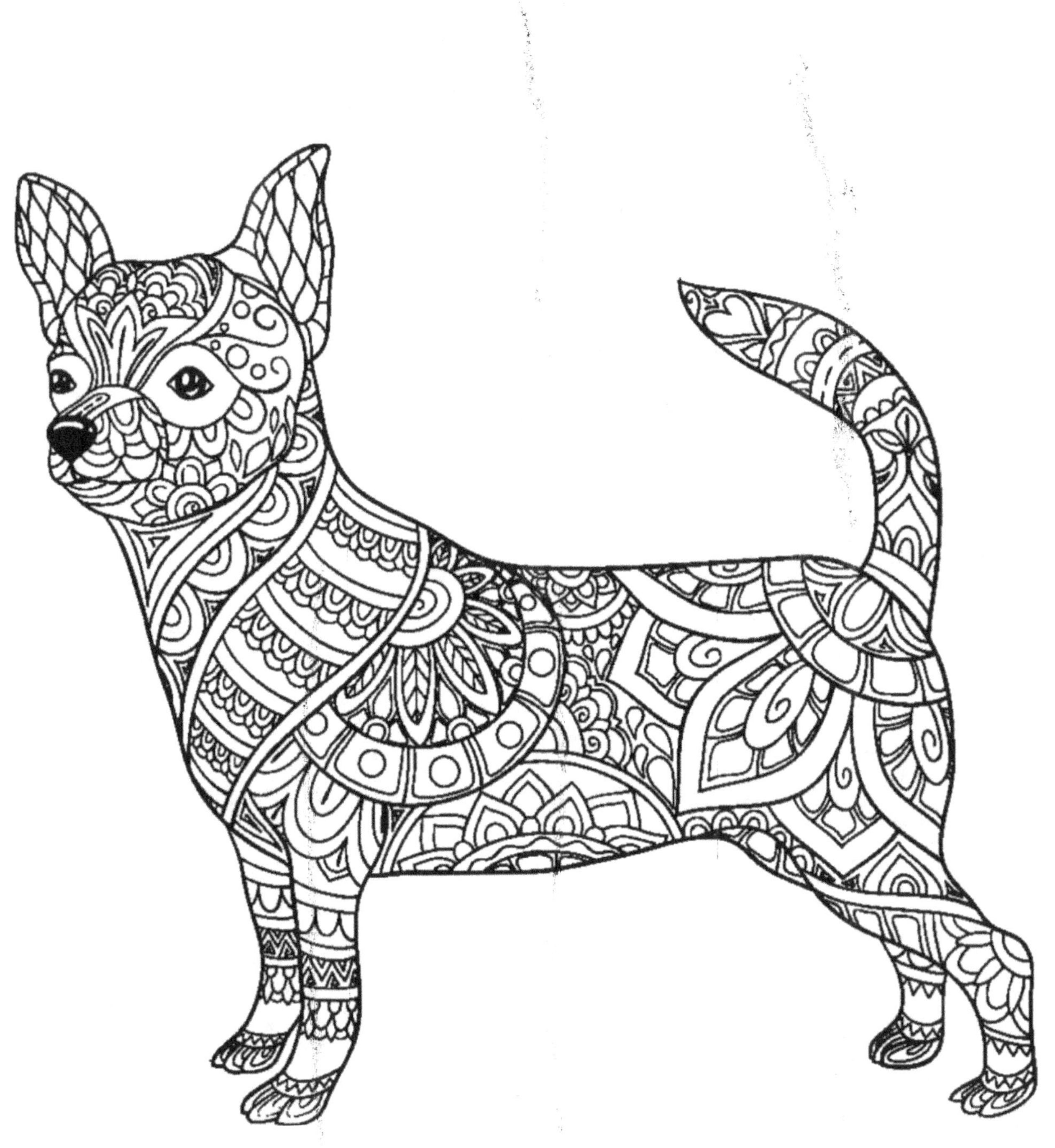

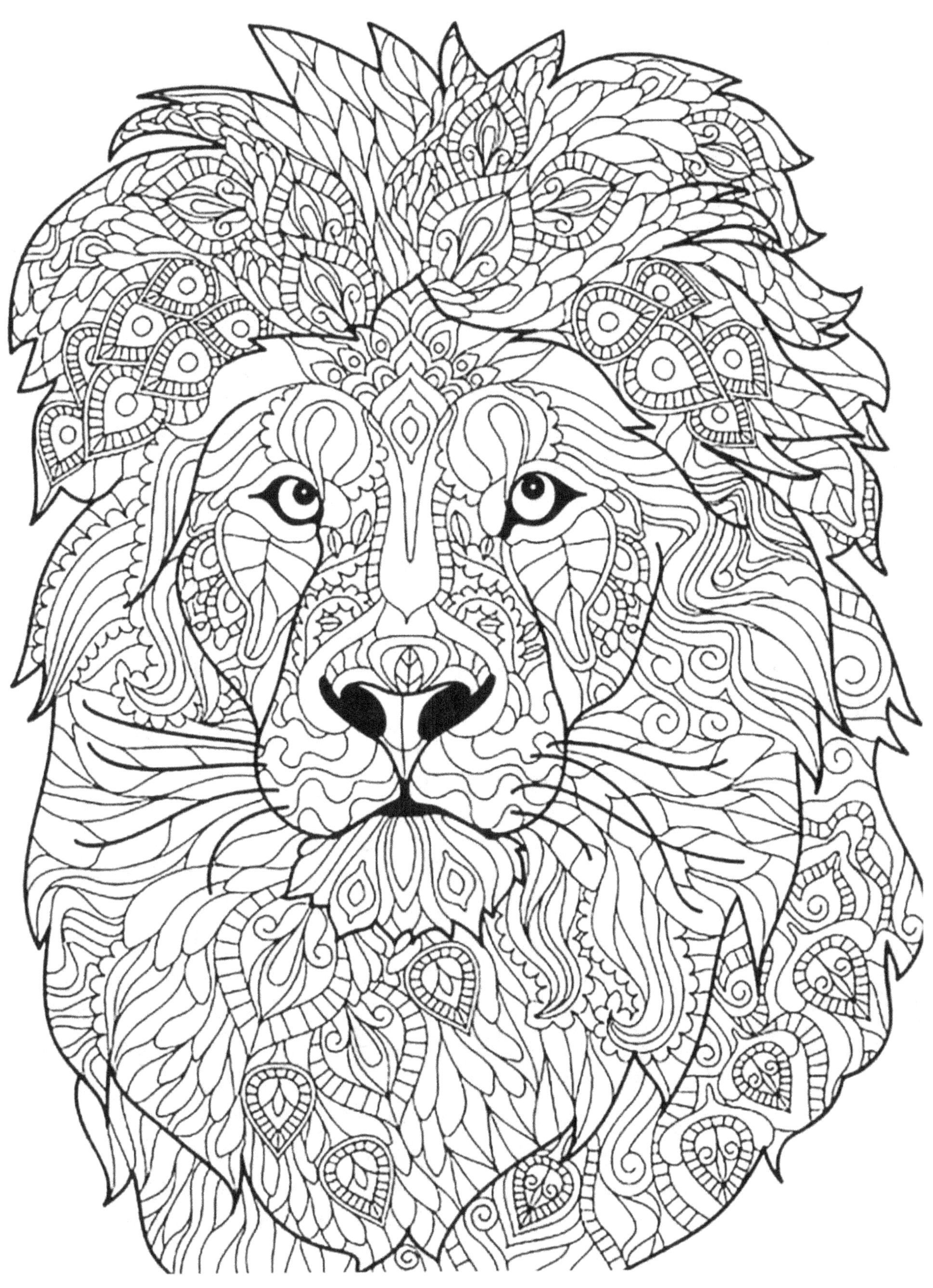

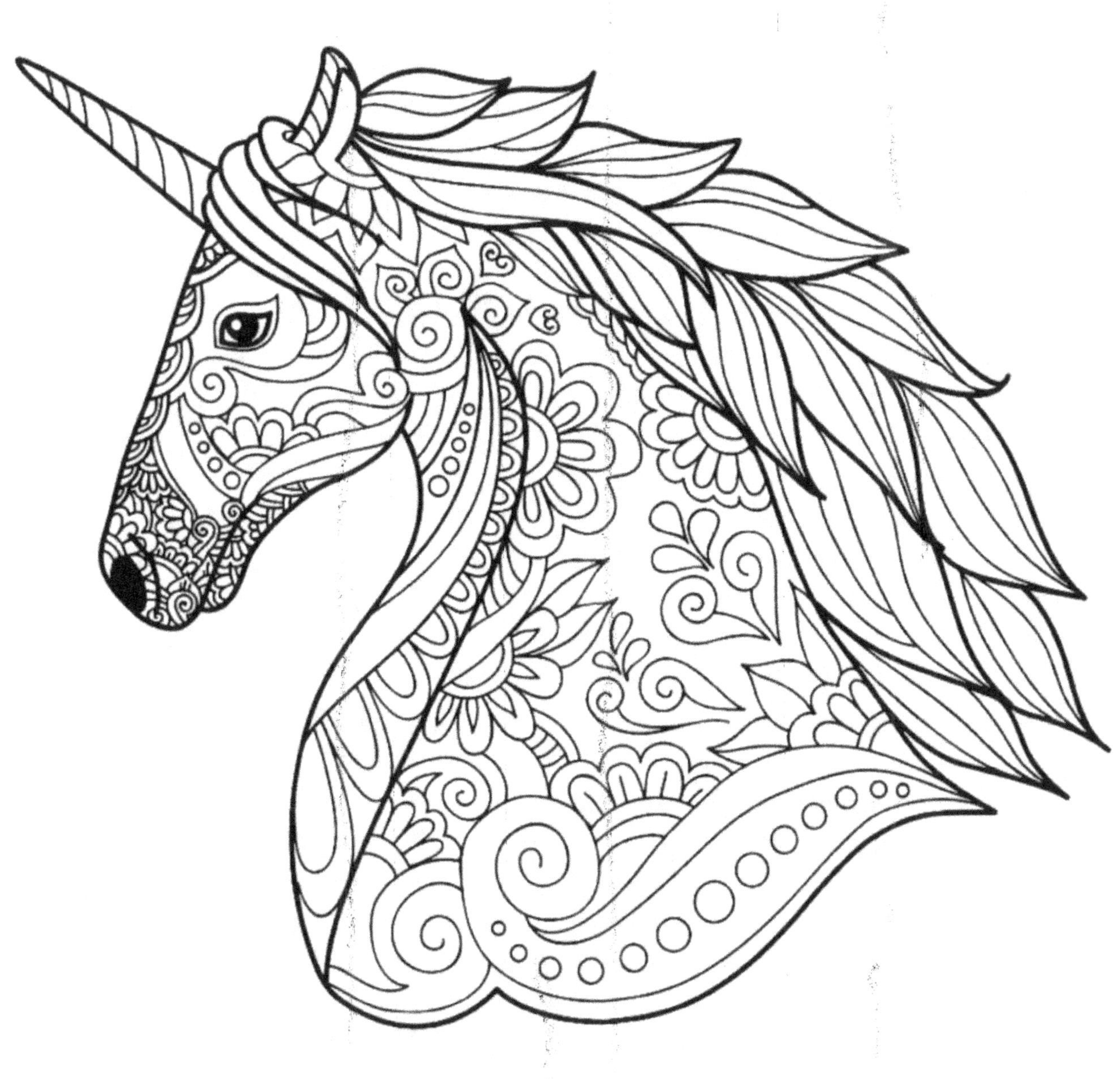

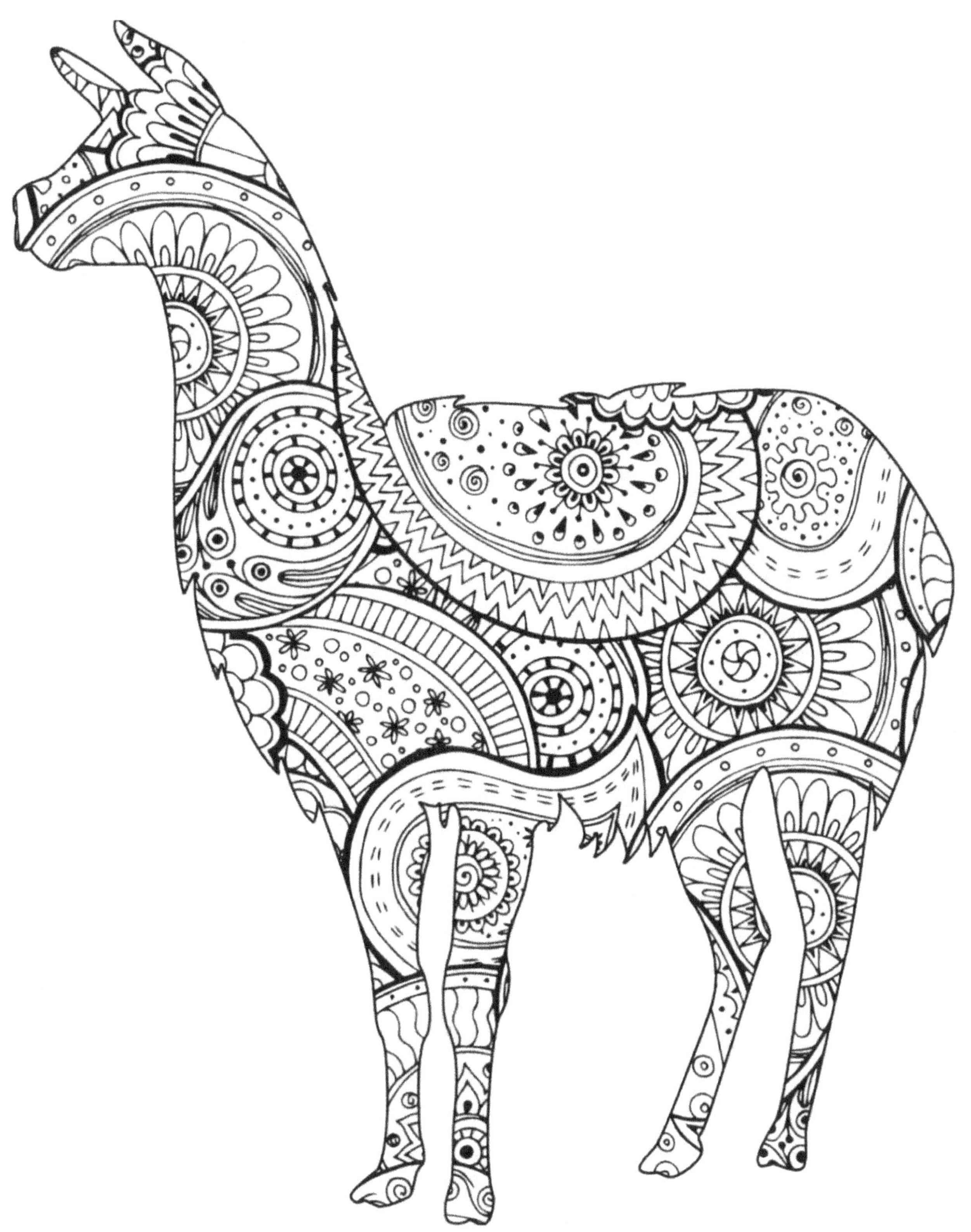

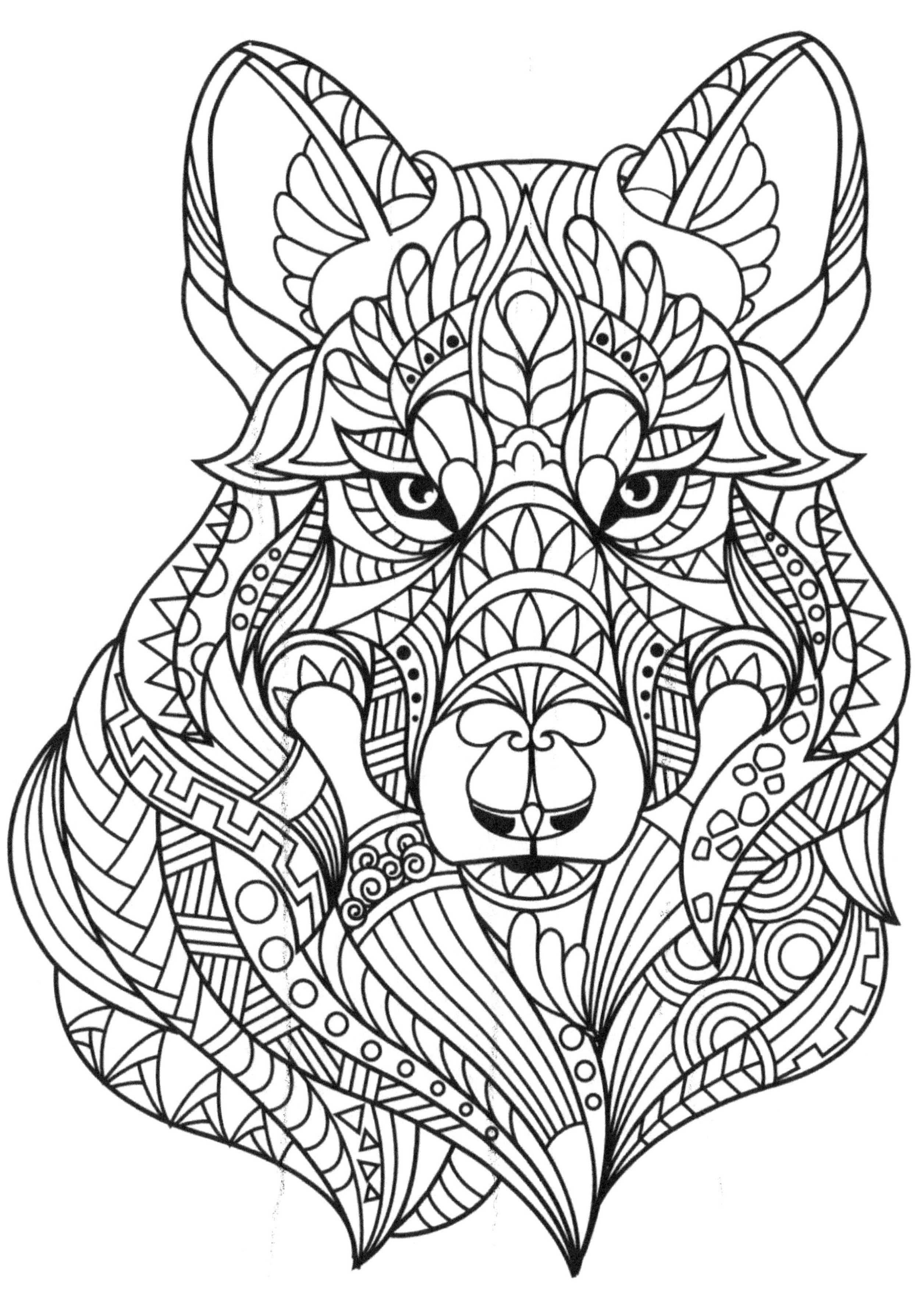

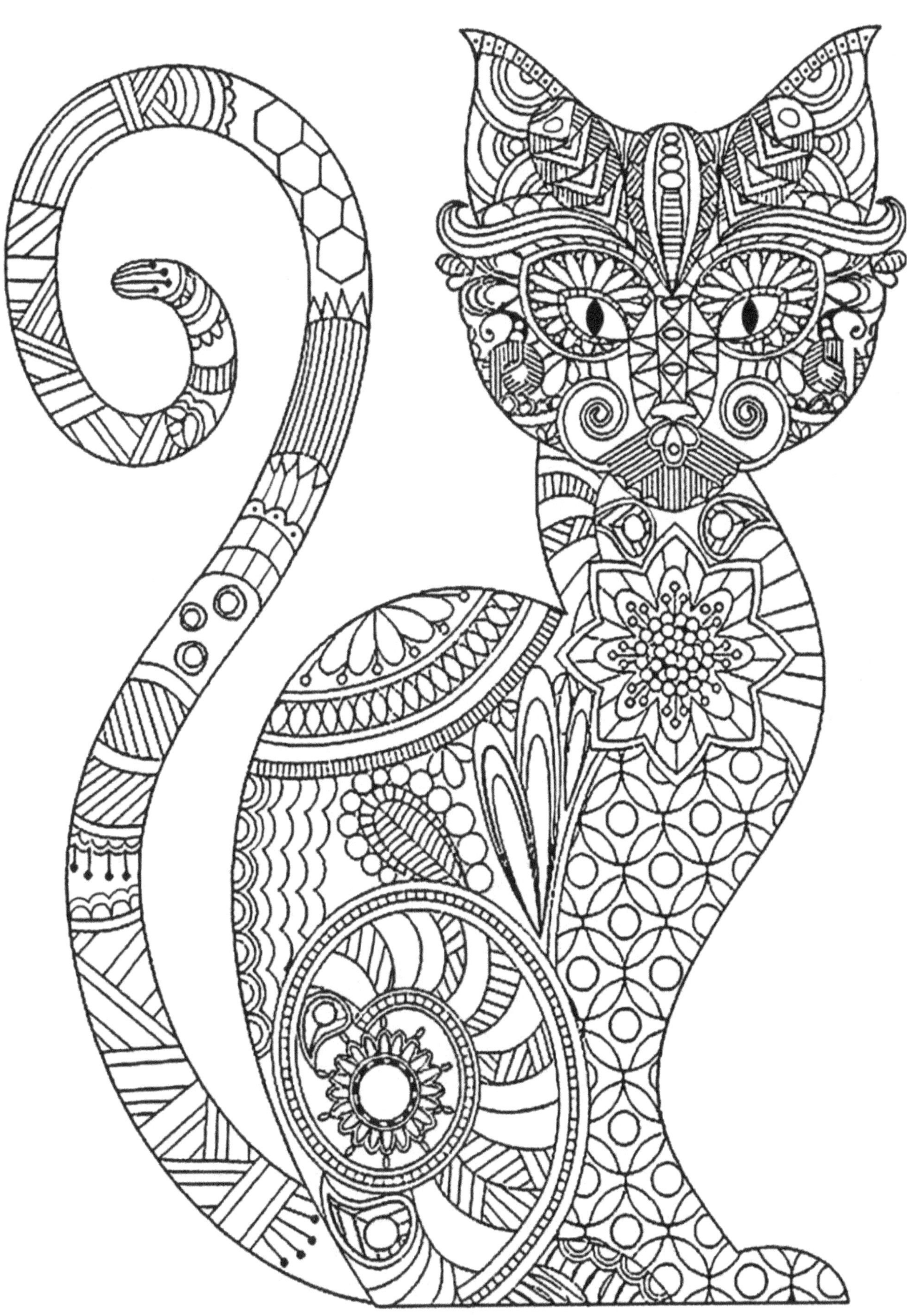

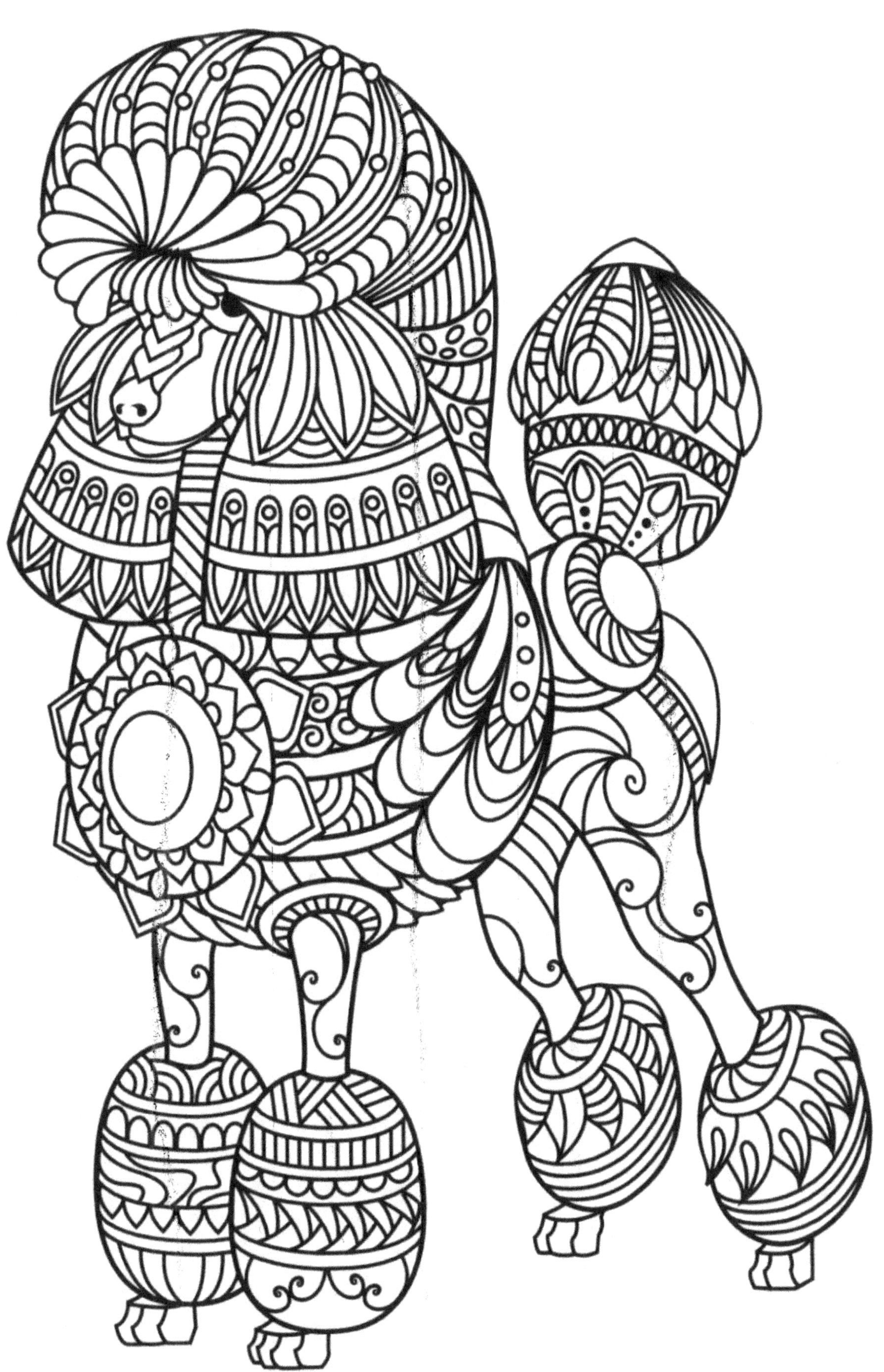

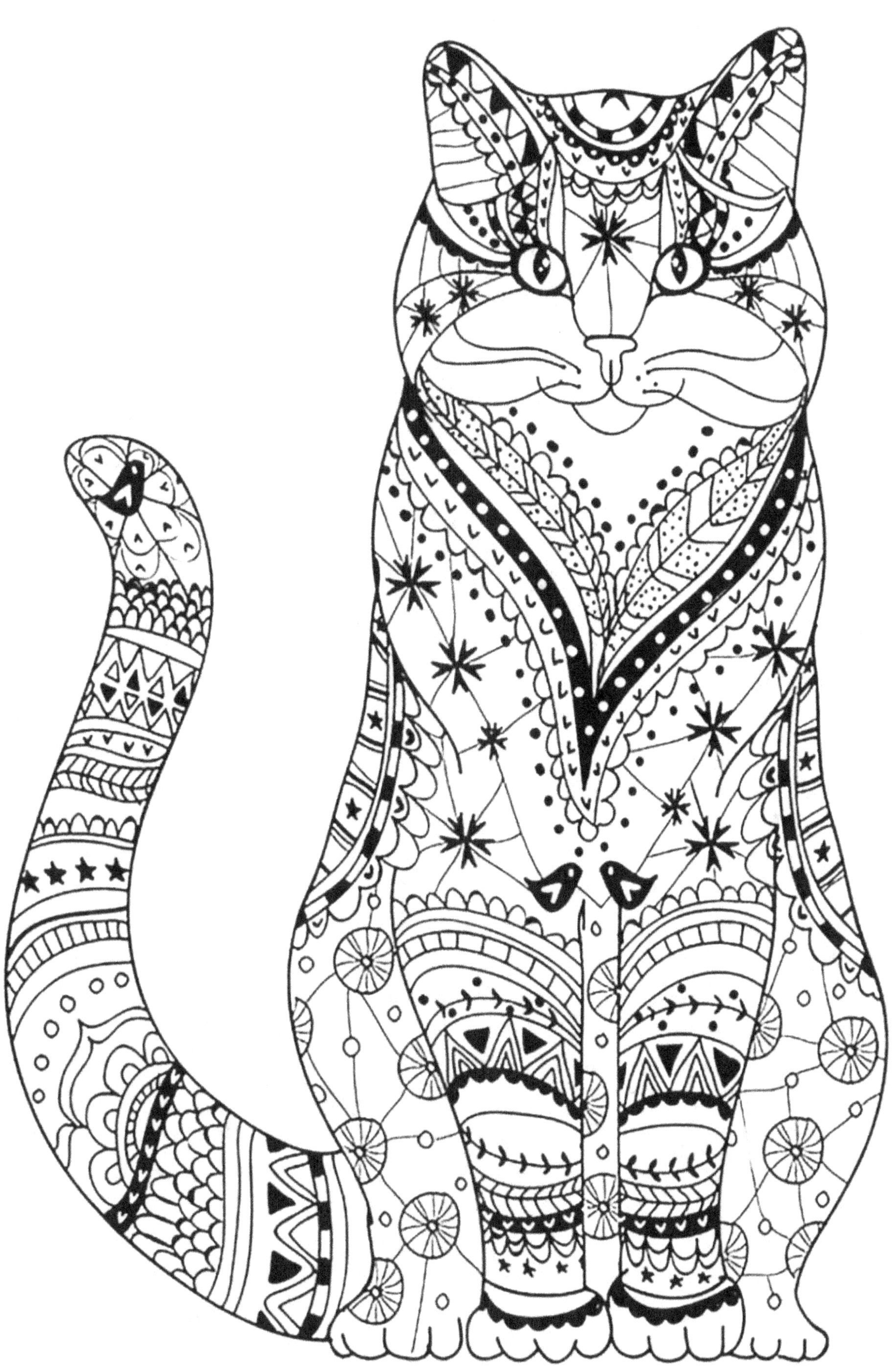

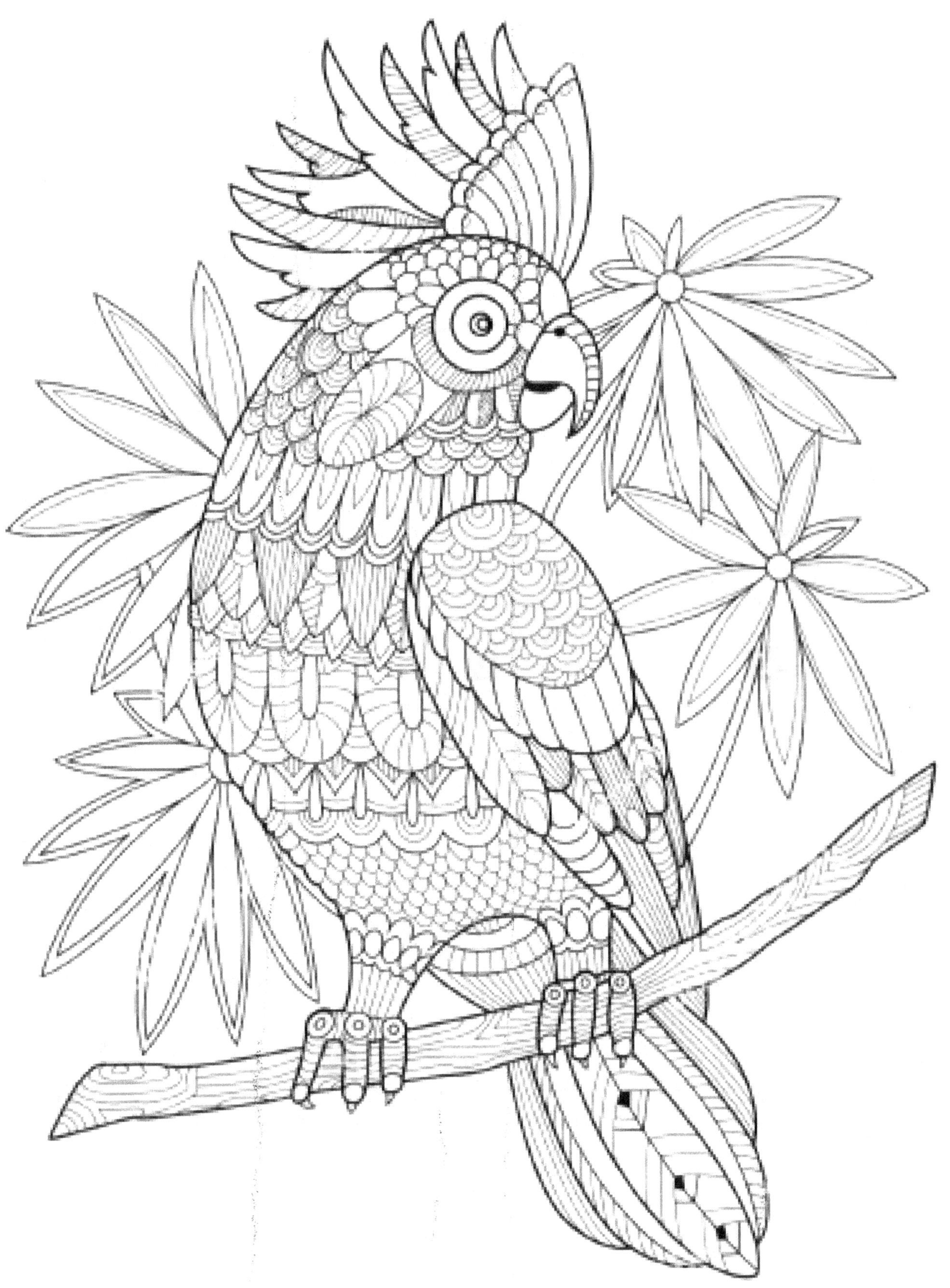

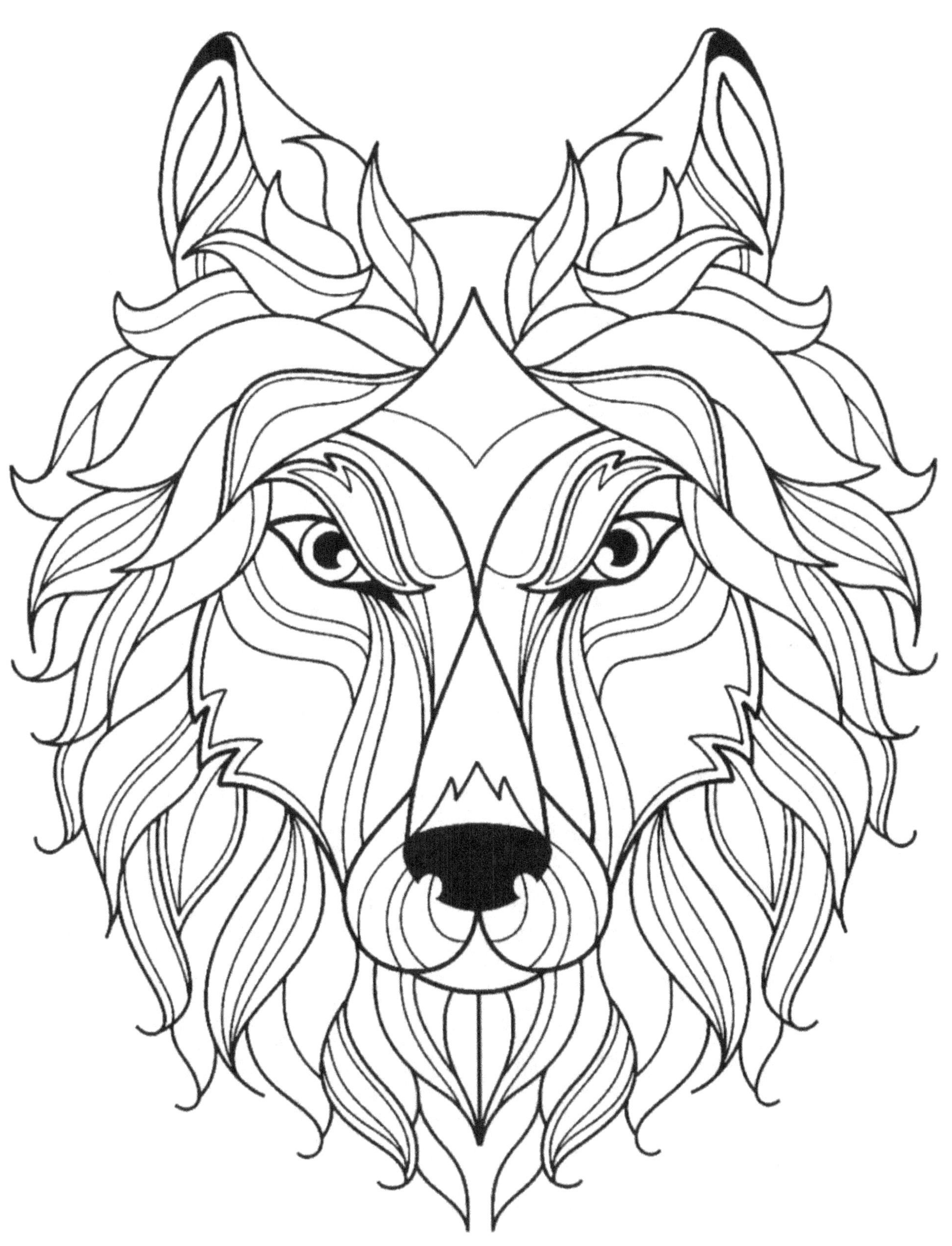

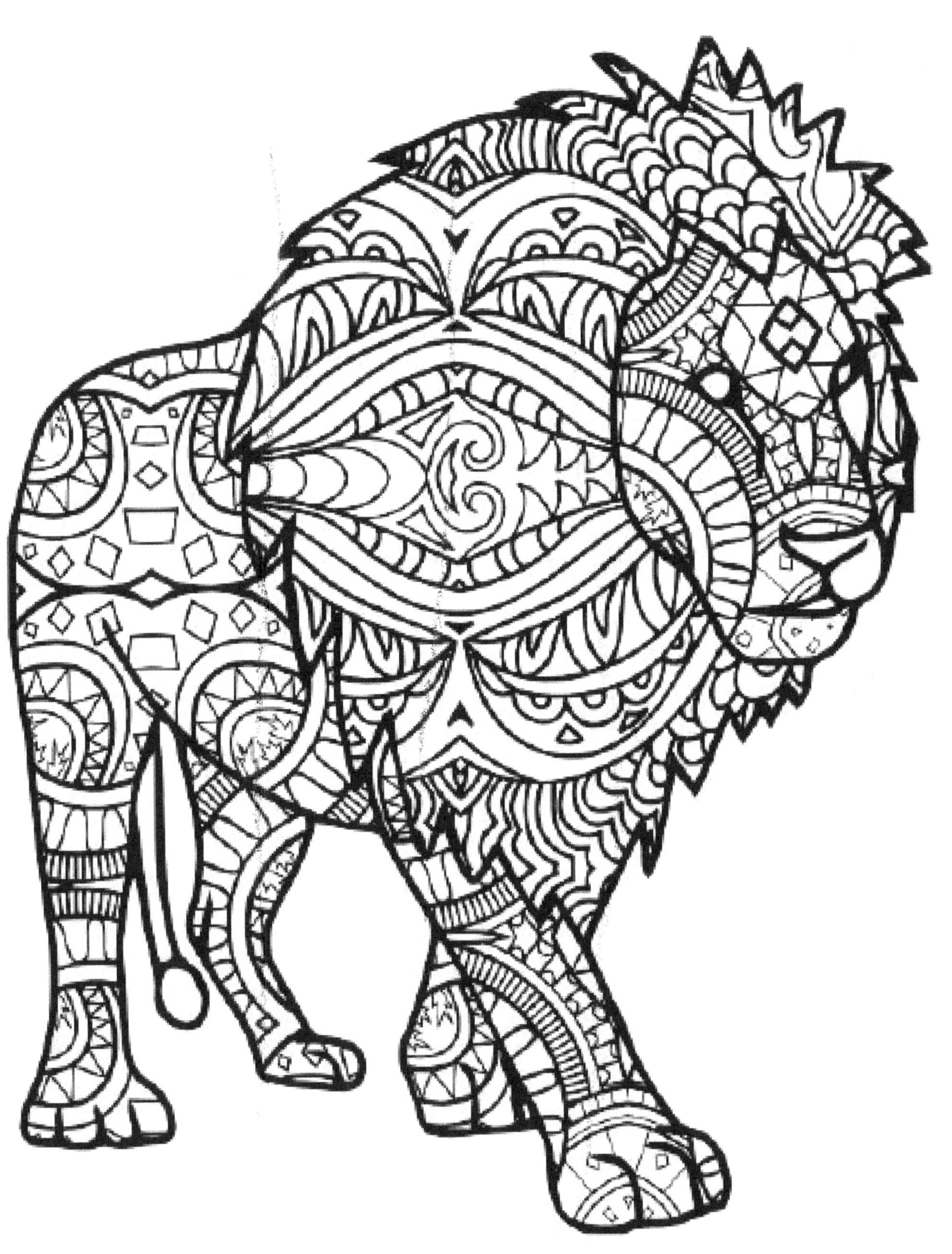

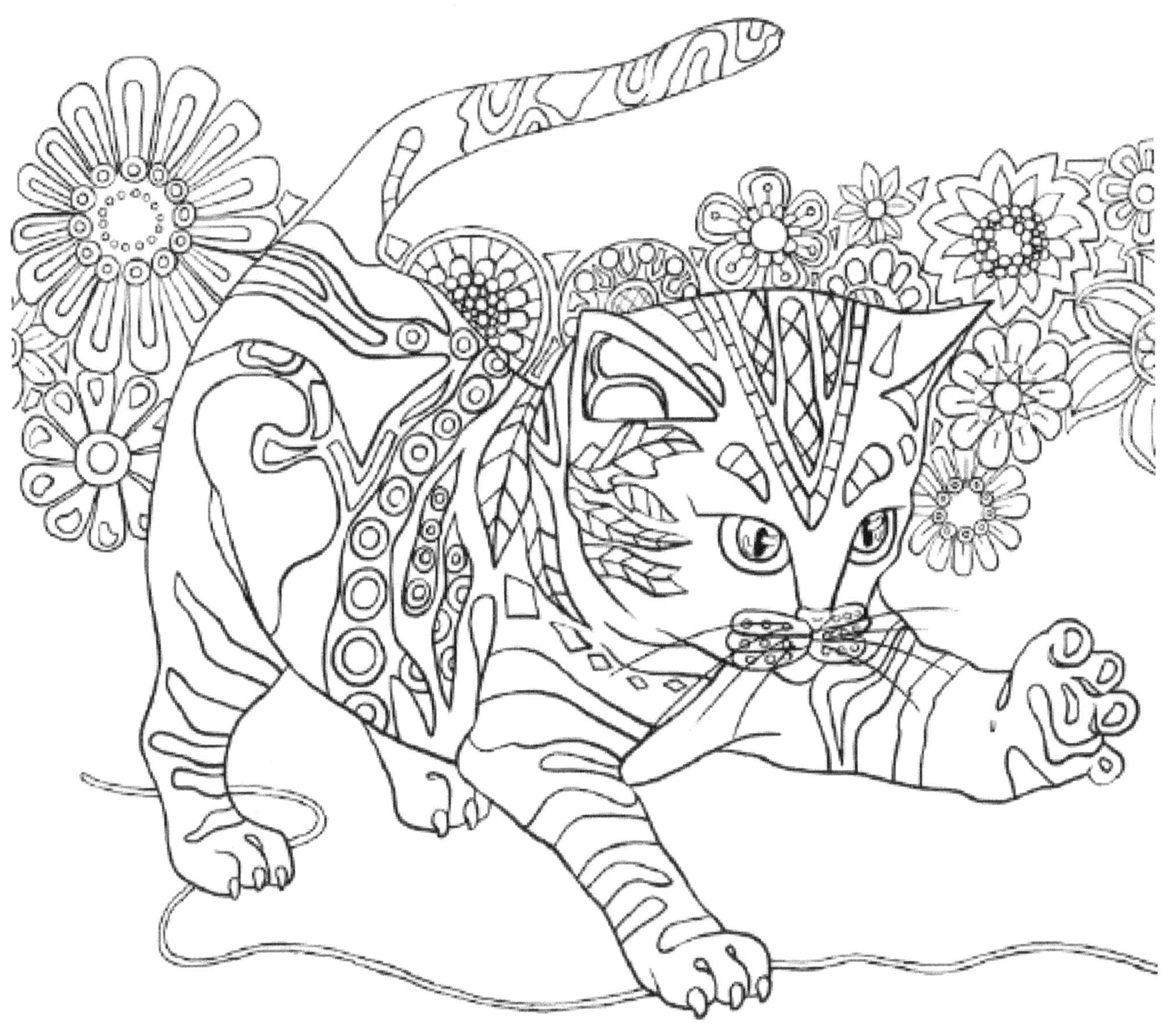

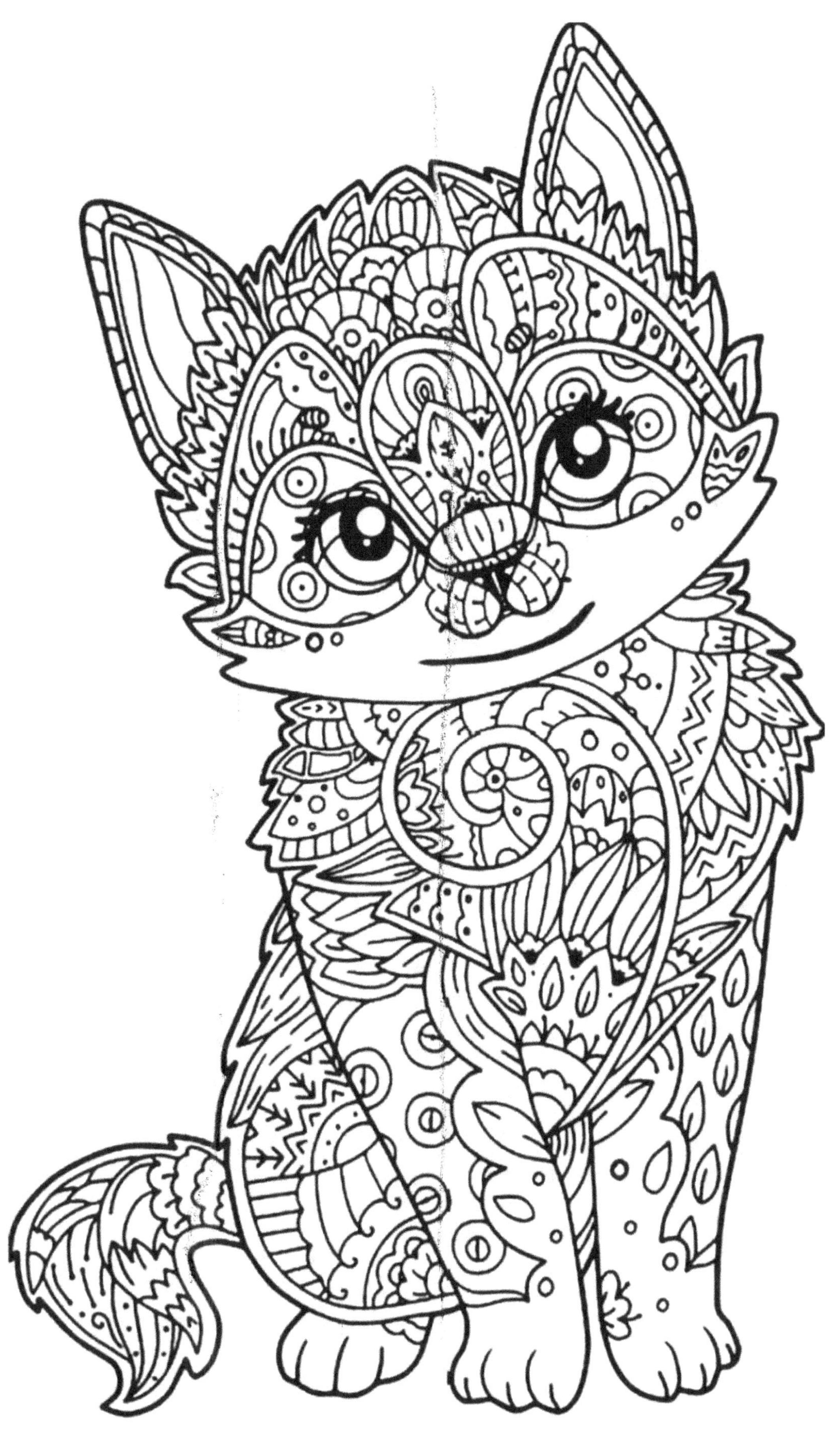

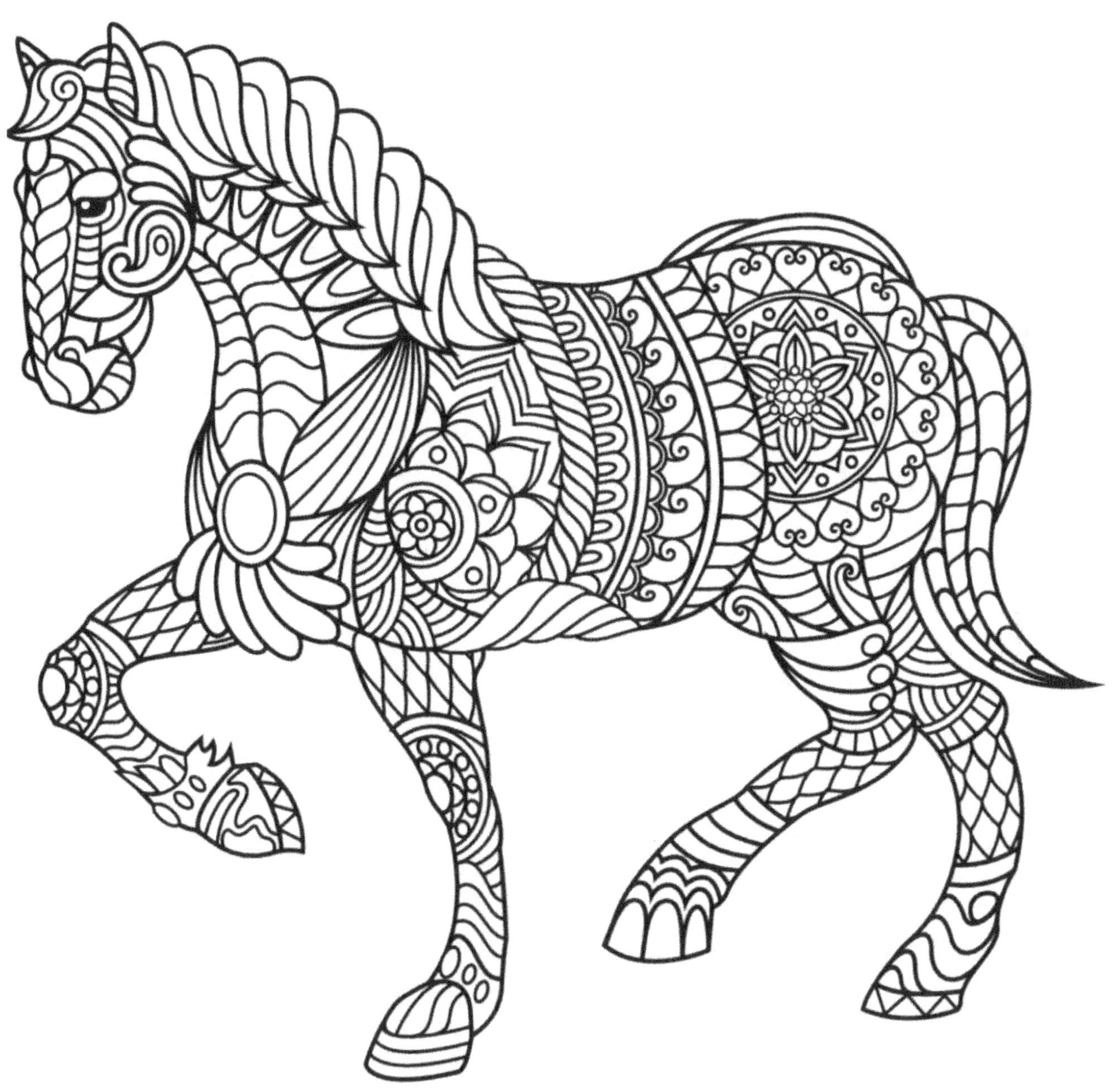

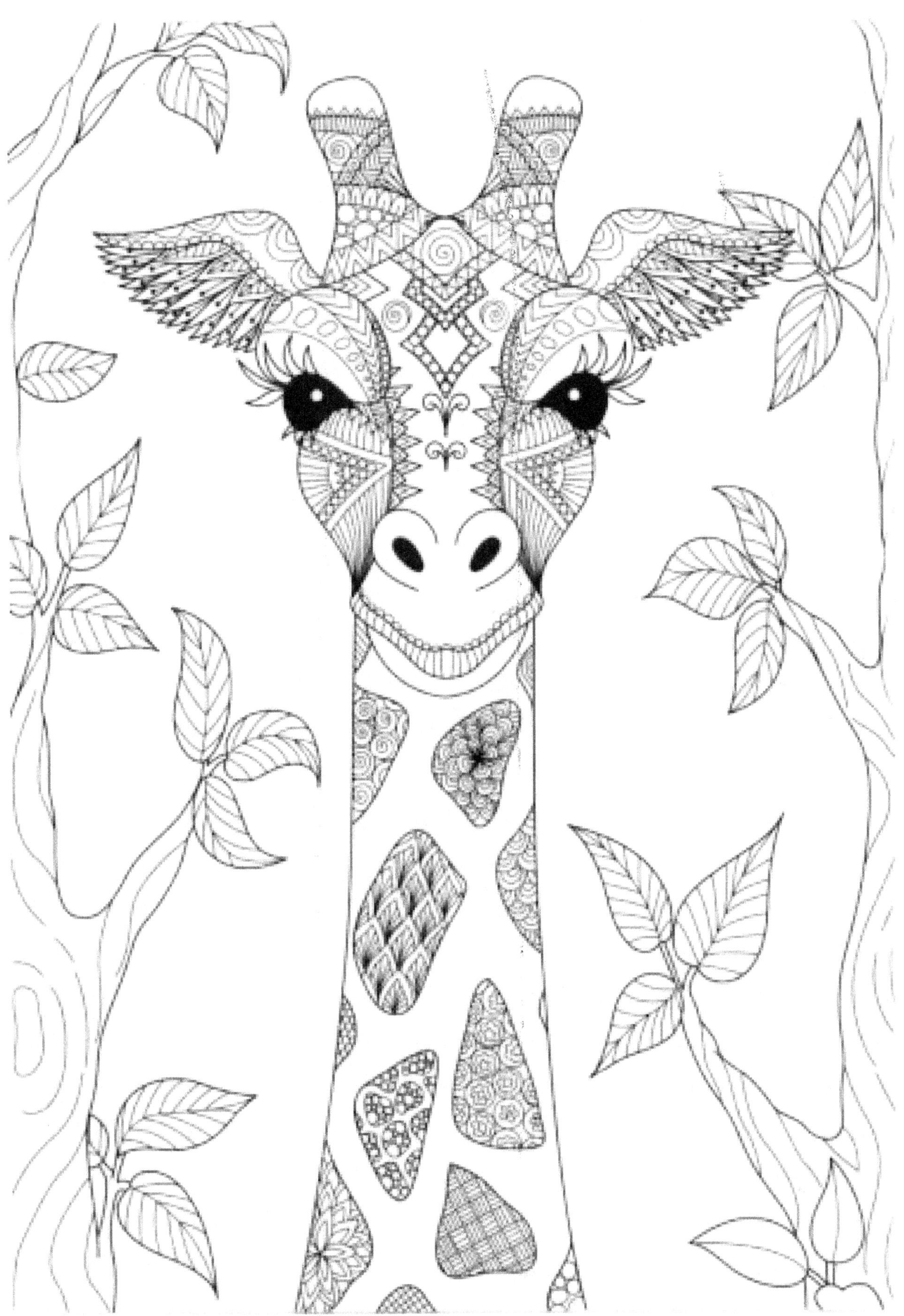

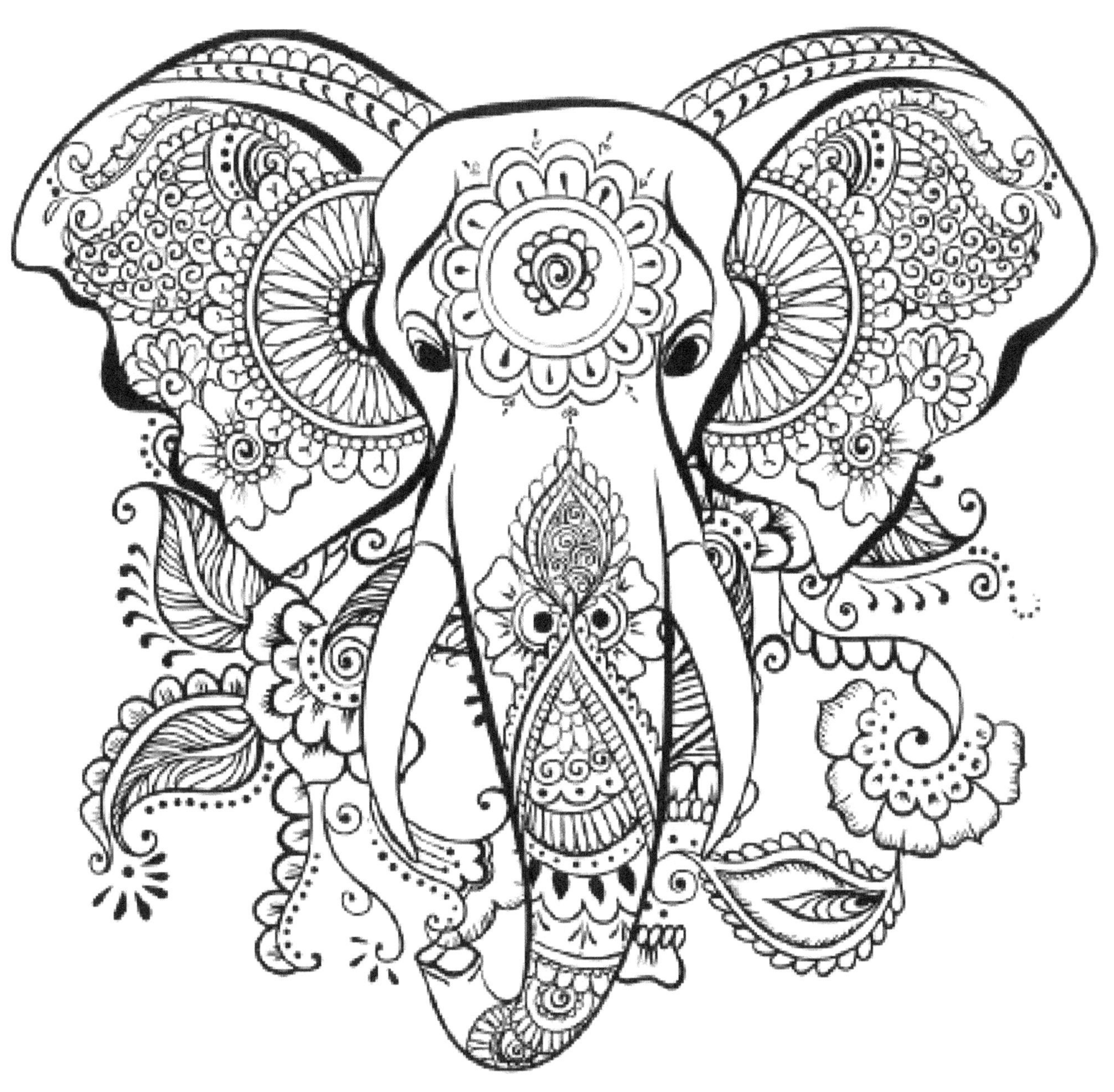

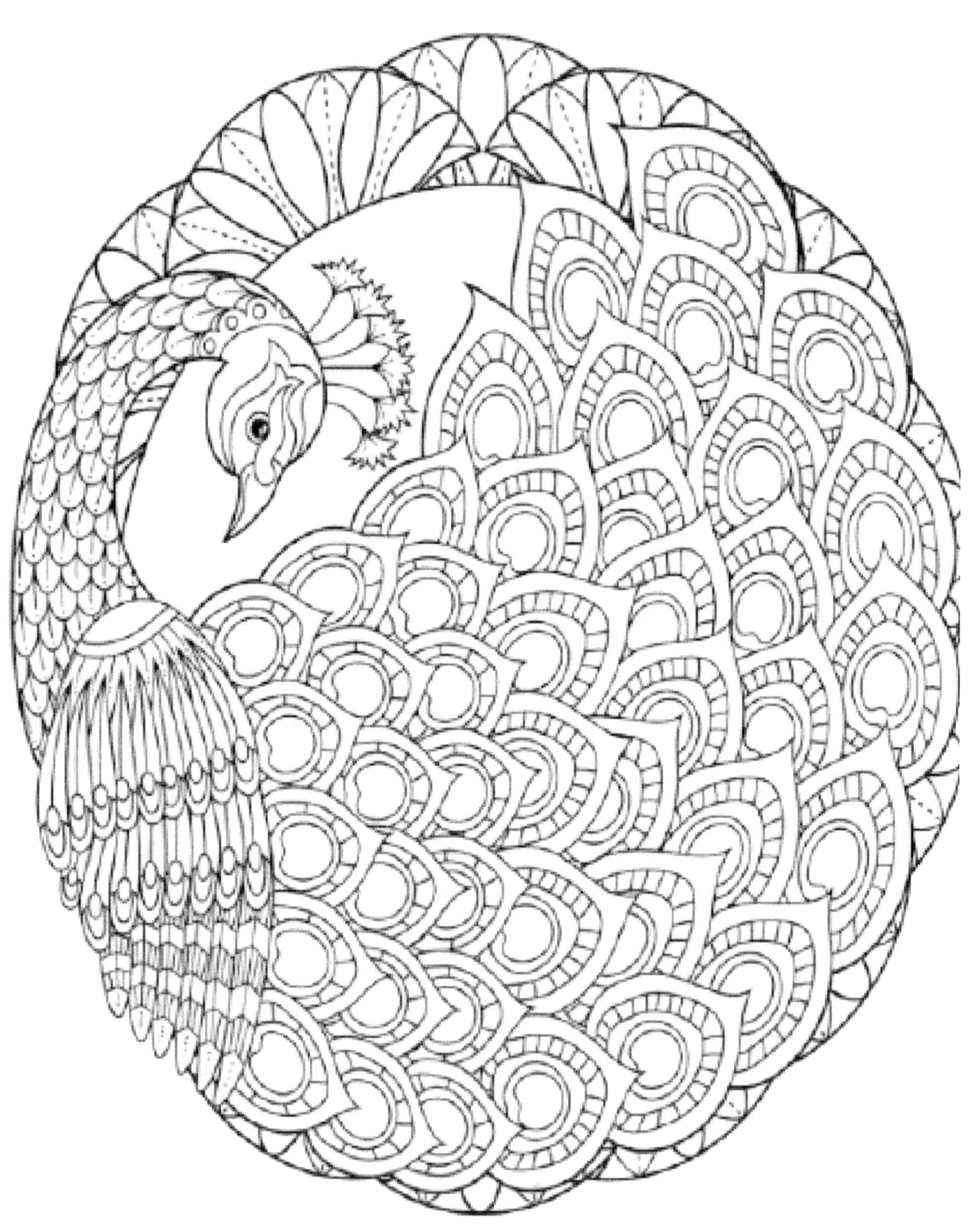